THIS HEART
WITHIN ME BURNS
CRISSY ROCK

THIS HEART WITHIN ME BURNS

CRISSY ROCK

From bedlam to Benidorm

FOREWORD BY KEN LOACH

JOHN BLAKE

Published by John Blake Publishing Ltd,
3 Bramber Court, 2 Bramber Road,
London W14 9PB, England

www.johnblakepublishing.co.uk

First published in hardback in 2011

ISBN: 978 1 84358 343 1

British Library Cataloguing-in-Publication Data:

A catalogue record for this book is available from the British Library.

Design by www.envydesign.co.uk

Printed in Great Britain by CPI Mackays, Chatham ME5 8TD.

3 5 7 9 10 8 6 4

Papers used by John Blake Publishing are natural, recyclable products
made from wood grown in sustainable forests. The manufacturing processes
conform to the environmental regulations of the country of origin.

Every attempt has been made to contact the relevant copyright-holders,
but some were unobtainable. We would be grateful if the appropriate
people could contact us.

Praise for *This Heart Within Me Burns*

'A book that will have you laughing and crying in equal measures. An incredible, honest account from an incredible, honest woman.'   *Ricky Tomlinson*

'An inspirational book from a genius of our time. A remarkable account by a woman who has had more kicks in the teeth than 17 Shane McGowans but still managed to pull herself up from the floor, stand tall and shout, "Here I am."'
                                                              Ken Scott

'A graphic and honest account of an incredible life, by no means over. Thank goodness it found the light of day.'
                                                         Trevor Dalton

Dear Mum and Dad,

It seems strange writing to you both this way but I am sure
you will get to read this one way or another. I don't have
to say I miss you because you already know that.

There were many times I took you for granted when I was
younger because I always thought you would be here forever.
I needed to write this down in my book to let my readers
know how special you both were. What you couldn't give us
in material things you gave us twice as much in love, and
you cared for us all like the best parents in the world.

I hope you are both together now, setting up a little home
in heaven. One day, one by one, we will all join you again.
It is why I do not fear death.

My brothers and I talk about you often. We say that we
never knew what your dreams were, because you lived your
dreams through us. Hopefully, as you look down on us,
you will see that our lives have become an extension of
your lives, filled with an abundance of love and honesty,
the same love and honesty you gave to us all.

Until one day when I'll see you again, I miss and
love you both.

CONTENTS

ACKNOWLEDGEMENTS

To my five beautiful granddaughters, you have given me the greatest joy my heart could ever have, and you have all inspired me in every word on every page. I love you lots, my jelly tots.

Thank you to my two daughters, Tracy and Hayley. There were many times I got it wrong as a mother, but never once did I ever stop loving you. I tried my best to protect you from the sort of life I'd experienced. At times I became overprotective. I love you both and I am so proud of you both.

Thanks go out to my four brothers, for always being there for me and allowing me to tell the stories in this book, stories that are so personal and so very, very special.

To my stepmum Linda, thank you for the years of love you gave our dad, me and my brothers, and for still being around to this day whenever we need you.

To Gill and Tony Gustafson who helped me along the road to becoming Crissy Rock. Without your support and love I don't think I would have ever made it. And of course to Kenneth Earle, my agent – the first man who treated me like a lady – and to Lyn and Tom Staunton who found me right at the beginning.

To John. The only time I ever feel like I belong to someone is when I am with you. Thank you for making me feel so special, so loved, so wanted and for never letting me give up. I love you more than you could ever know.

To big Dee and Margaret Anderson, my beautiful Belfast friends, my surrogate parents who always cheer me up no end whenever I see you both.

To Gerry and Deemo Povey. Gerry, you are my hero, my domestic goddess and my friend. Your kindness and friendship throughout the years has been a blessing; and, Deemo, never change your answering-machine message; it makes me laugh so much. Not forgetting Carol Spence and family who took me in and treated me like one of their own.

And last but by no means least, to Margie Jones. What can I say, Margie, thank you for our friendship over the last 28 years. Margie, we've laughed and cried together, you've been the big sister I never had and the best friend anyone could ever ask for. I truly love you to bits. x MIZPAH – The Lord watch between me and thee when we are absent one from another.

Oh my God, and I nearly forgot, there's some fellow called Ken Scott. He came to meet me outside the UK Bar in Benidorm and said he was interested in seeing my scribbles and ramblings that he had heard someone talking about. I said to him, 'You cheeky get, that's my life you're talking about!' Ken and me hit it off straight away. The fact we were as cheeky as each other made us get on like a house on fire.

I had been trying for years to get a book together but something always felt missing; it was never going to happen.

ACKNOWLEDGEMENTS

The lack of education and knowledge of the written word held me back, and I knew that my spelling left a lot to be desired. So we got together and he held my hand along the way; he taught me that grammar was not just something for school and, yes, at times, he damn well bullied me. But, more than that, he persuaded me to talk about things I hadn't wanted to talk about. And slowly, as it began to take shape, I could see that it all made perfect sense.

Ken has had me laughing and crying and helped me make sense of the pages and pages of my words that eventually became this book. Without his expertise as a writer, his gentle powers of persuasion and the ability to discipline his subject, they would have stayed stuck in the drawer of my bedside cabinet forever. He helped me open up the words on each page like a picture, giving it depth, a vision... meaning. And now it's eventually all come together, it seems strange flicking through the pages of a story that has been my own life. So Mr Ken Scott ... Scotty, from the bottom of my heart, I can't thank you enough for your patience and understanding, and your skill in helping me to become a writer.

Thanks also to Ken's editor (and mine too) Carol Cole – my first experience with a schoolteacher since I left school, and may I say what a pleasant experience it was. A true professional, Carol – thanks a million.

And finally to Derren Litten and all the cast and crew in Benidorm who put me back on my feet again.

FOREWORD

BY KEN LOACH

Crissy Rock is a remarkable woman and she tells a story that would break your heart. We met, as she describes, through a mutual friend, Ricky Tomlinson. We were casting a film called *Ladybird Ladybird*, written by Rona Munro, based on a true story of a woman whose life was wrecked by abusive relationships but who was unable to escape the stereotypical way she was seen by others. I think Crissy and I met several times during the casting. Each time the truth of her responses in the imaginary scenes we set up became more impressive.

Throughout the filming, her energy was prodigious. We would shoot emotional and disturbing sequences for maybe 10 hours or more. Behind the camera we would all be quite drained. Crissy would clap her hands and demand to know where the action was to be that evening. Like all good actors, she communicates directly, eye to eye, with the others. Her reactions are instinctive and authentic.

As Maggie Conlan, she was touching, not only because she

was vulnerable but also because she was a fighter. It was her refusal to be beaten, despite all the unspeakable disasters that happened to her, that moved the audience. Of course, those qualities are not only true of Maggie Conlan, they are true of Crissy herself. To survive her early life she needed great resilience but to come through with wit and a warm spirit shows a strength that is quite extraordinary. I cannot think of anyone I have worked with who shines more brightly.

I hope Crissy's demons are finally vanquished. But, partly because of them, may she continue to astonish us with her work.

PREFACE

BY KEN SCOTT

I first met with Crissy Rock in the spring of 2009. Soon after our introduction, I watched her perform on stage at the UK Cabaret Bar in Benidorm on Spain's Costa Blanca. Her performance onstage that evening was full of energy, her timing close to perfection, and she had the audience eating out of her hand. She was clearly at her brilliant best ad-libbing and verbally counter-punching with a few brave souls who dared to make their presence known to her. Her act was clearly not scripted and I likened her ease and confidence, her storytelling ability and her wisecracking to one of my favourite comedians, Billy Connolly.

A few days later, I agreed to work with Crissy over a trial period of one month, to see if we could pull together her life story into a marketable autobiography. She supplied me with 23,000 words of her musings and ramblings she'd collected over the years. I could see immediately that Crissy was dyslexic and had clearly struggled to construct the sentences and paragraphs. But shining through the pages like a beacon were the words of someone who could not only tell a story but also tell it sincerely and with an enormous amount of honest, raw emotion.

No matter how hard life had kicked Crissy Rock in the teeth, she always bounced back, and had the incredible ability to drag humour and positivity out of any situation, no matter how desperate or dire it seemed.

She told me modestly that she had done a little acting. Her award-winning performance in *Ladybird Ladybird* brought me to the verge of tears and I marvelled at her performances in such films and TV series as *Dockers*, *Brazen Hussies*, *Springhill*, *Hero*, *Born to Run*, *Butterfly Collectors*, *Trial & Retribution*, *The Factory*, *Closure*, *Nice Guy Eddie* and *Night Collar* as I watched many of them over and over again on DVD.

Her talents didn't end with acting. When I visited her at her modest home in Benidorm, some amazing paintings adorned her walls, ones that I felt should be on display in galleries in London, Paris or New York. I commented that they must be worth a fortune and asked if she had insured them. She smiled as she pointed to the signature on each one: the moniker of Crissy Rock herself…

I watched more of her stage performances in Benidorm, and one night, at the end of her act, she broke out into a stunning rendition of 'Simply The Best' that floored the audience. As she finished, she turned to face them and said, 'You didn't know I could sing, did you?'

They didn't. Neither did I.

Crissy Rock is a genius, of that there is no doubt. As I strive to perfect my chosen art of writing, she breezes through four skills – comedienne, actress, artist, writer – with consummate ease, an incredible achievement. However, what makes her so special are the barriers and obstacles she has had to overcome in order to succeed. She is undoubtedly one of the strongest characters I have ever had the pleasure to work with. For Crissy, this book was an enormous help in coming to terms with the demons that have plagued her throughout her lifetime. It not only represented closure for her, but also could demonstrate to others that, despite everything that life can throw at you, if you have the belief in your own ability and love the person inside, you can overcome anything. She is living proof of that.

I want her to know that I love her to bits and have enjoyed every second of her company during the construction of this quite remarkable book. Now that our project is complete, I hope our friendship continues and I have the chance to work with her again.

INTRODUCTION

There was a time when I couldn't read a book, never mind write one. But, once I had learned to read and write, I used my basic writing technique to exorcise my demons. I read voraciously, anything and everything I could get my hands on, and tried to emulate the great writers by scribbling down notes, mostly in the middle of the night after a bad dream: a special blend of my own ramblings and philosophy that would hopefully stick around for many years to come, long after I'm dead.

To write this book, I purchased a laptop computer that helped with the spellcheck and grammar, although half the time it didn't know what I was trying to say, never mind spell it for me. I would wake up from a particularly bad nightmare and would then batter away for hours on the keyboard until daylight came. You, dear reader, will share those nightmares with me during the course of this book.

I wanted to write this book for my children and grandchildren, no one else. I want them to understand why I have sometimes made mistakes and bad decisions along the way. I want them to realise that anyone can rise like a phoenix from the ashes. Often it isn't easy, in fact it's bloody difficult, and, every now and then, you need a little luck and an odd break here and there. I want this book to capture hopes and dreams, and show anyone who reads it that humour can rise to the surface, no matter what the circumstances. I am no one special, just an ordinary person who once had a break that changed my life, and laughing through the tears helped me cope.

So join me on my journey of sadness and joy, and of triumph and pain, and accompany me through the alleyways of my life, during which I somehow changed from Christine Murray into Crissy Rock.

PROLOGUE

A pain like fire ripped across the whole side of my jaw and I became aware of a deafening noise tearing through my ears. My whole body seemed to lift off the ground and, within a split second, I was lying dazed in a heap on the floor.

It didn't stop there. My husband threw himself on top of my near-unconscious body, raining blows about my head and body. The ordeal only lasted a minute, maybe two at the most, but it seemed like an eternity.

When it was all over, I heard the front door slamming and was overcome by an eerie silence, broken only by my own sobbing and sniffling, and my heart beating as fast as I'd ever known. I ached everywhere. I just lay there in total confusion, aware of some warm, sticky, wet liquid across my face. As I touched it, the liquid oozed through the gaps between my fingers. I cried like a baby until I could remember crying no more.

I fell asleep, and, when I woke again, it had gone dark. At first

I thought I'd slept through a nightmare, but the overpowering smell of stale blood filled my nostrils. Whether through cold or shock, I was shaking like a leaf. I tried to get my head around what had happened, and, pathetically, thought for a moment or two that I may have been to blame.

My head was thumping, as if a drum was pounding inside, as I dragged myself on to all fours, and then groaned as I struggled to my feet. I walked gingerly to the bathroom, where I turned on the light.

Who was that girl in the mirror?

Whose was the disfigured face staring back at me caked in dry blood, bruised and battered beyond recognition?

When he finally came back, he acted like nothing had happened. He dropped himself into his favourite armchair and turned on the TV. I stood like an idiot staring at him. He had the cheek to say, 'What are you looking at?'

'Have you seen my face?' I asked in astonishment.

'What about your fuckin' face? It's still as fuckin' ugly as when I fuckin' married it.'

My mouth fell open. I couldn't believe what I was hearing and why there were no apologies from this monster sitting before me. Where was the man I married? Had his personality changed, or had there always been an ogre inside him, ready to be unleashed?

My lip trembled and I felt like bursting into tears all over again. I felt I could cope with the physical hurt he'd inflicted upon me, but with those few well-chosen words he'd torn my heart into a million pieces.

I had to get out, had to go... right there and then. I turned to walk towards the door.

'Where the fuck do you think you're going?' he sneered from his armchair.

I didn't reply. I just kept on walking. Before I could escape, he was up on his feet in a flash and caught me.

'You're going fuckin' nowhere, you fuckin' slut.'

He grabbed my hair and pulled me back, balled his right hand in a fist and propelled it towards me, catching me on the side of the mouth. I felt my jaw crack, and two of my teeth fell towards the back of my throat. I flew through the air and landed on the threadbare carpet. Lying on the floor, I managed to gather the fragments of teeth from my windpipe and spat them out. As I gazed at them, lying in a pool of my own spit and blood, I heard my husband growl, 'From now on, you do as I fuckin' say. Is that clear?'

I whimpered like a stricken dog and apologised to him. I actually fucking apologised to him!

'I'm sorry,' I said. 'I'm sorry... sorry... sorry.'

Those words still haunt me to this day.

CHAPTER ONE

HERE I AM

Since then, at an uncertain hour,
That agony returns,
And till my ghastly tale is told,
This heart within me burns.

I was born on 23 September 1958 at Sefton General Hospital. It was on Smithdown Road, in the Liverpool 8 area of the city.

My mum's name was Margaret and she was 20 years old when I was born, only five foot tall with brown hair and eyes that changed from blue to green in a certain light. I could never figure that one out but I swear by almighty God they did.

Dad and Nan used to say that Mum suffered with her nerves. She would disappear off to the hospital every now and again for treatment, sometimes for weeks at a time. Those damned nerves attacked her for years, but I didn't understand then what nerves were. Sometimes she would shout, 'Move – you're getting on me bleedin' nerves!' and yet we were standing nowhere near her! And sometimes Dad would shout out the same thing, as would Nan and little Nin too, but they weren't supposed to have 'the nerves' so how could we get 'on them'?

(I'd better explain. Little Nin was actually me dad's nan, not my nan. Dad had grown up thinking that 'little Nin' was his mother, but my own nan – Ninny Lizzie – who he thought was his sister was actually his mum. Nan was only 16 when Dad was born, so little Nin (his nan) brought him up as her own son. She called him Teddy, so because her last name was Ash, Dad was known as Teddy Ash, even though his real name was Eddie Murray.

God, I'm confused now and I'm part of the bloody family.)

Anyway, back to my mum. She was funny, a lovely woman who, it was said, would never hurt a fly. I'm not surprised: if one came within a foot of her she went bloody hysterical, screaming blue murder. If I ever asked her why she was so afraid of such a small creature, she would reply, 'It's me bloody nerves, girl.' Those damned nerves again.

She could be such fun. Her dancing eyes could sparkle like the crown jewels. She would spend hours making up games with us, and playing hide and seek. Well... playing seek at least, because, as you'll discover, we had nothing in the house to hide behind. But, whenever her nerves returned, she'd withdraw into herself for long periods, like she was lost.

Dad, five foot seven and very handsome, worked as a coalman for Buller Mills Coal, at a coal yard just off Crown Street. He met Mum while she was babysitting for a friend of his, Maggie O'Hare. He married Mum in March 1958 at St Nathaniel's Church, after she found out she was pregnant with me. Six months later, in September, I was born. Mum has described the wedding as a low-key affair; not only were the two of them brassic but my dad was just getting over the shock of finding out that his 'sister' was in fact his mother. (Nan and little Nin... remember?)

Married life for Mum and Dad found them at Mum's mum's two-bedroom flat on the fourth floor at 11D Windsor Gardens, in one of Liverpool 8's many tenement blocks. If anybody asked us where we lived, we'd reply, 'With me nan in Liverpool 8.' It was perfectly normal back then for a young couple to start their married life under their parents' roof or, if not, with an older sister or brother. The plain fact was that they didn't have enough money to furnish their own place, but they hoped that, if they lived cheaply and saved money, they might eventually afford furniture for a house of their own.

It was only a two-bedroom house and, when I was young, I slept with my nan and granddad in a big, lumpy but cosy bed that seemed to take up most of the room. I'd sleep next to the wall, and snuggle up against Nan in the middle of the bed, while Granddad slept on the outside. Today, sleeping with your grandparents would be considered a little strange, but back then it was perfectly normal. Also, in the depths of winter and with no heating in the house, I'd still be as warm as toast. I was one of the lucky ones; a girl I used to go to school with shared a bed with five others!

I don't remember an awful lot of details about my early life, but I can recall the arrival of my brother Brian, who was born on 5 February 1960. Brian and me were very close. I don't remember us ever fighting, but, there again, I suppose we must have done sometimes. I mean, all brothers and sisters do, don't they?

Our Brian was always a live wire. He loved sugar butties, and I blame all that bloody sugar for giving him the energy. One of my earliest recollections was of him standing at the table nearly drooling as Mum sprinkled the sugar on to the bread. At the same time he would tap his leg and twitch.

It drove our mum crackers trying to get him to stop. But he never did, and the more excited he got, the worse it would be.

As soon as Brian was old enough, I introduced him to the incredible adventure playground that was the streets of Liverpool 8. At the time, the Liverpool council had decided to move people out of the area's many slums, and so there were lots of derelict houses waiting to be pulled down. These houses were dangerous, and therefore the greatest play areas in the world, so I wasted no time in introducing our Brian to them. Every time we went into a house we shouldn't have been in, I got goosebumps on the back of my hand. Brian would just stand there with his gob open, twitching and tapping his feet.

One game we played in those houses was inspired by an amazing film I saw on TV one day: something called *Wuthering Heights* written by someone Brontë. What a daft name, I thought, but, as I watched from the floor of our darkened lounge with my head propped up against the settee, I had an idea. I almost felt I was the heroine up on the moors, and so, whenever Brian and me went inside those derelict houses, Brian would call me Cathy and I would call him Heathcliff. Come to think of it, Heathcliff was a daft name as well.

We kept our games in those houses secret, and prayed that Mum would never find out. If she had known we were playing there, she would have had a canary fit and ragged us both good and proper. When Brian wasn't thinking straight and called me Cathy at home by mistake, my heart was in my mouth at times.

Sometimes on Saturdays we would have to stay in, especially if Mum had the nerves. It was as if she didn't want to let us out of her sight. Meanwhile, Dad would be watching the horse racing on TV and would yell at us to be quiet. 'I've got a bet on it,' he'd say. I'd stare and stare at the horse, wondering what that meant, but Dad would never explain, so engrossed was he in the horse and the race it was running.

We knew if we made a noise we'd be chucked outside to carry on playing, so Brian and me would devise a plan to have a fight, during which one of us would start crying.

'Stop crying,' he'd shout, 'there's me bets down again. You're putting the mockers on them. Get out and play.'

It never failed. It was even worth getting a clip round the ear sometimes if we could go and be Cathy and Heathcliff again. When Dad hit us, Mum would shout, 'Stop hitting them on the head. That's how Larry died in Curly, Larry and Moe.'

The streets in those days were great fun to be in and nobody worried about little kids being out on their own. We didn't need mobile phones, you just got yelled in. In any case, I would later find out that greater dangers lurked behind the front door of our own house.

Any old rope we found in the derelict houses would be used to make a swing for us outside. Brian would shin up the street lamp posts made of iron, and in no time would tie the rope around the top. He was the best climber in our gang, like an energetic little monkey, and we'd always give him first shot on the swing when he came down. We'd tie bits of stick and old tyres on to the bottom, anything, as long as our arses could get a grip. If we couldn't find anything to use as a seat, we'd tie a big knot in the bottom of the rope.

Brian would make the most of his first swing and we'd have to drag him off. He'd stand waiting, impatiently tapping his foot. 'It's me turn now,' he'd shout again and again until it really was his turn again.

Some of the other kids got pocket money but not us. It wasn't fair, but Dad's reasoning was 'Life isn't fair', so we'd earn our pocket money by other means. Help was at hand thanks to the Armey and Layfields factory, situated behind our tenement block. Once a week, for some strange reason, a man would stand on the factory roof and throw down wooden boxes with drawings of oranges on them.

'Fuckin' good firewood, dat,' someone would always say and we'd gather in gangs at the bottom. All the kids used to stand looking up, shouting at the men on the roof.

'Hey, mate.'

'Down here, mate.'

'Over 'ere, pal.'

As the boxes tumbled, we would squeal and run away, to avoid getting clobbered. I swear those factory workers aimed for us sometimes but we didn't care. Then, once the boxes hit the ground with an almighty crash, there was a big free-for-all and we'd scurry back to grab as much wood as we could. Sometimes, we'd fight with the other gangs to make sure we'd collect enough to make some money.

Then we'd tie the bundles up and drag them through the streets to one of the derelict houses where no one could see us. We'd sit around snapping the big bits of wood with our feet against the bottom step of the wooden staircase, making them into smaller bundles. Sometimes we'd use a half brick and batter the wood into even smaller pieces which always filled out the bundles of kindling. It was so much fun and worth every splinter we got in our hands and fingers.

To carry around our wooden bundles, which we would sell for a penny or whatever anyone would give us, we'd send Brian to fetch his stirrey. A stirrey was like a cart made of wood that, if you were lucky, had two big wheels at the back and two smaller ones at the front. Brian's stirrey was an integral part of the business and that made him proud.

The firewood business was a good one to be in as a kid. Sometimes people would give us empty milk bottles as payment. They were worth a penny if you returned them to the dairy. We'd also get paid with lemonade bottles. Those were like gold dust: you got three pennies for them by returning them to the local corner shop. Gradually, the stirrey would fill up with bottles as the wooden bundles were sold and, after a trip to the dairy and the corner shop, our pockets were full. Who needed pocket money?

Once we'd received our payment, we could spend our earnings at Tunnel Road, home to the picture house. We loved going to the flicks. When the curtains opened, the whole picture house would start cheering, but the first Saturday we ever went, Brian began to cry when the cheering started as he didn't know what was happening. He cried that much I had to take him home, by which time I was crying myself because I knew I'd missed the film too and the bloody woman at the picture house wouldn't give us our money back.

Our Brian was always nervous, even when he was little; he had a nervous laugh that would turn into a cry. But I didn't mind him crying. I could never get angry with our Brian. When he started to cry, I would grab his hand and say, 'Come on, shut up, you're all right now.' I would put my arm around his shoulders and he'd stop. Not only was Brian my brother, he was my best friend too.

The next week, after another bumper time for our firewood business, I'd take Brian back to the picture house. The pictures would always start with a sweaty, suntanned man banging a gong, and then the titles appeared on-screen. As he bashed his gong three or four times, that was the signal for Brian to get excited and start tapping his foot again. We watched all sorts of films but mostly cowboys and Indians. Brian loved those the best.

In the summer, Mum and Dad would take us to the park at weekends and, sometimes, as a real treat, on the ferry across the water to a place called New Brighton. I thought we were going to another country but later we found out it was just across the other side of the River Mersey.

When the ferry got to the other side of the river, it was like a big free-for-all. Everyone would be bustled up, eagerly waiting for the ferryman to drop the gangway so we could all get off. He had to make sure everyone was behind a metal strip so the gangway wouldn't hit anyone. He'd be like a man possessed, waving his hands and shouting, 'Calm down! I'm doin' not'n until you calm down and get back!'

So we'd all shuffle back and nod our heads and stand patiently, as if we were in the school dinner queue. The ferryman would wait until everyone was calm and quiet. Then, as soon as the gangway had dropped down, it was like the bloody Dunkirk landings. Everyone would rush off to get to the beach first. Everyone wanted the best spot and to have as much time on the beach before they had to head back and catch the last ferry back to Liverpool.

Me and Brian would play on the beach, collecting shells for Mum, and building sandcastles that were the strangest and oddest shapes because we never had a bucket or spade. We'd use our hands and empty tins and cartons that we'd find on the beach. Then we'd rush back to Mum for jam butties. Those great days out always felt endlessly warm and sunny, and I can remember sitting on the back of the ferry as we waved goodbye to New Brighton, wishing we could live there forever.

CHAPTER TWO

LIVERPOOL 8

The ship was cheer'd the harbour clear'd,
Merrily did we drop
Below the kirk, below the hill,
Below the lighthouse top.

At that time of our lives, everything seemed so cosy; we never gave a thought to any dangers in the street or who or what could be lurking in the derelict houses and we'd never heard of paedophiles or murderers. The only bad men we'd heard of were Ole Nick and Spring Heeled Jack. Mum would say, 'Don't go wandering off or Spring Heeled Jack will get you' or 'Don't be naughty or I'll send you to Ole Nick.'

Occasionally, you would hear of a burglary or a mugging, but that was big news and very rare. We were brought up to know that the people who did such things were bad. Mum and Dad drilled into us what was right and wrong. We had a huge loving family and loads of friends and, even though we didn't have any money, in many respects we were the richest kids in the world. I would never have swapped those first six or seven years of my life for all the tea in China.

Nan, who we lived with in Windsor Gardens, was called Henrietta, but everyone called her Hetty. She was dead funny.

She too was very small, only five foot in her stocking feet, and she had a lone gold tooth set in her false teeth which glistened whenever she smiled. I have a picture of her in my head standing in front of an open fire laughing at some funny story she had relayed, her gold tooth sparkling like a beacon as her head lolled backwards, and not being able to speak for laughing so hard. Apart from her gold tooth, a worn thin wedding ring was the only other gold thing she ever owned.

I remember her long fair hair and her constant singing. Her pride and joy was an old stereogram that stood on legs under the window and looked like a bloody big coffin. Her favourite singer was the country and western artist Jim Reeves, and she played his records morning, noon and night. I don't know if she had any records of other singers but if she did they'd never come out of the box. Her favourite Jim Reeves song was 'Welcome To My World'. More often than not, as I came in from school, it would be playing. As I came through the door, she would always have a smile for me.

I can still hear her now, saying, 'Hello, me little one. D'yi wanna join me in a dance?'

I'd smile and nod, and run over to where she stood grinning with her arms held out wide. I would step on to her slippers and she would waltz me around the room singing along word-perfect to 'Welcome To My World'. I'd squeal with laughter as she closed her eyes and lost herself in her dreams. She'd open them occasionally to make sure we weren't heading for the fire then screw them tightly shut again as quickly as she could.

If I hear that song today, it still brings a tear to my eyes and I am there, back in Liverpool 8 as a six-year-old dancing with my lovely nan in the living room in my safe and loving world. A travel company has recently adopted the song for its ads on TV and, every time it comes on, I have to fight back the tears.

I miss her so much. She was perfect in every way, and I loved her with all my heart.

I don't remember her ever shouting, even when she used to call me for my tea at nights. There was no need for her to raise her voice – it was as if her voice had the perfect pitch to make it heard.

Nan's skin was like silk apart from her hands that were as rough as a docker's.

Nan did everything for all of us. She seemed to sense when she was particularly needed, when Mum's nerves were about to become overpowering. Nan seemed to clean from the minute she got up until the minute she went to bed. We had nothing, no fancy furniture or fireplace ornaments but, even so, what little we had always sparkled.

The step outside our house was always spotless too. Nan cleaned it with Vim at least two or three times a week and she'd even sand the stone a little to make a perfect edge. I can't understand how that step didn't disappear altogether. To look at Nan's perfect shiny step from the landing of the tenement block where we lived, you'd think we lived in a palace. It was an illusion Nan painted to the outside world until she could no longer get down on her hands and knees. She kept trying, of course, but then couldn't get up again and had to be physically lifted on to her feet. As I walk across that step in my daydreams, I can still remember the distinct smell of damp Vim.

There are so many smells I remember from those days, and most of them I associate with Nan. I can still smell the paraffin from the heater that was used in the winter and the carbolic soap that Nan scrubbed everything with... including us. There was San Izal, a black thick syrupy tar that bubbled white when it came into contact with water. She'd do the veranda with that, and the hearth with Zebro. I'd help her with the hearth helping to buff it up. It was black lead and Nan and me would finish up looking like Al Jolson. Then there were the smells from the washhouse, and I have another crystal-clear memory of watching her operating a manual mangle with the steam rising from the clothes, while singing 'Welcome To My World'.

I loved the trips to the washhouse, helping Nan pile the clothes and bedding into a huge sheet in the middle of the kitchen and tying it up into a big bundle. She would heave the washing on to the old washhouse pram and Brian and me would push from underneath. We'd run alongside the pram as Nan pushed it along the landing and we'd giggle and laugh in anticipation as we reached the stairs – we had to get the pram and washing down eight flights of them.

Usually, for such a job, you'd enlist family members and neighbours to carefully manoeuvre the pram down each step of each flight, practically carrying the pram down to the front street. Not our nan.

'Are you ready, Christine, Brian? Right, here we go!'

And, with a wicked grin and a quick check to make sure the washing was wedged tightly into the pram, she'd heave the pram off the top step of the landing.

The pram bounced and clattered down every step and the exercise was repeated eight times at the top of each landing. How the pram never fell to bits I'll never know but it didn't. Me and Brian would shriek with laughter as the poor thing groaned under the effort before finally coming to rest a few minutes later at the entrance leading out into the street. The neighbours would be cursing and shouting, but their raised voices were barely audible through the thick brick and plaster walls. Just as well the walls were thick: our nan's pram must have taken half a dozen inches of plaster from those walls over the years.

Once in the front street, Nan would be off as if she were in a race. We would try to keep up with her and, eventually, as Brian would be lagging behind, she would lift him up to sit him on top of the bundle and off we would go to the washhouse. Me and Brian would sit outside and play with the pram, taking turns to push each other up and down the street until Nan came back out again. We would be absolutely knackered and once again Brian, being the little one, would get the prime spot sitting on top of the clean washing, holding on to the huge knot of the sheet as if he were John Wayne on his horse riding across the screen of the Tunnel Road picture house, and there he'd sit smiling with a grin as big as the Mersey Tunnel all the way home. All simple memories of innocent fun-packed days.

I don't remember how old we were when Mum had another baby. It was a little girl called Janet but, from the beginning, even though I was just a child myself, I instinctively knew something was wrong, very wrong. Janet was born at home, while Brian and I played on the front landing. I heard my nan say she had been born very ill, with her nose bleeding, and they couldn't stop the blood. I remember everybody being upset but didn't understand what was happening to my new sister. The very next day, the vicar came and she was christened. I was happy because the vicar was obviously there to tell God to make her better and then everything would be fine again. But the vicar looked so sad and sombre and I didn't quite understand that. Had God not answered his prayers?

Janet died a day after she was born, but we never really knew what 'dead' was. Death was never discussed with kids and we were always just told if someone had died they were away to see baby Jesus. Why was everyone so sad? I wondered. I'd love to see baby Jesus.

Mum never really got over Janet's death. She had the nerves all over again, only this time they were even worse. There were no more days in the park or ferry trips to New Brighton. Instead, Mum started taking us to Smithdown Road Cemetery where Janet was buried. But, because there had been no money for a funeral, she had been buried in an unmarked grave without so much as a little stone with her name on. It was like she never existed. What was that all about? The council deliberately punished people with no money, stopping them from grieving. The evil, wicked bastards.

We'd still go to the cemetery looking to see if we could find the grave our sister was in. Mum would wander around in a daze, checking every headstone convinced that we would find one with 'Janet Murray' engraved on it. Meanwhile, me and Brian would pick daisies, dandelions and buttercups to put on graves with no headstones just in case Janet was buried under any of them. There was a little comfort for Mum in knowing her baby was close by, yet she also knew she could never sit down beside Janet's grave and mourn. The pain in our mum's heart was unimaginable and eventually wore her down. In the following years, she seemed to spend more time in hospital than she did at home.

After a couple of years, Mum fell pregnant again, and this time gave birth in hospital to a fit and healthy baby boy called Ian. He was a chubby little thing with a big mop of black hair and it seemed to be just the tonic Mum needed. So we were back to being a normal family again.

As he got a bit older, Mum would let us take Ian out in his little pram. Letting two small kids out with a three-year-old would be unheard of these days but back then it was perfectly normal. Liverpool was like one huge family and you didn't just have one mum: the whole street was your mum looking out for you and making sure you didn't get into any trouble. Everyone knew everyone in the tenement blocks and streets of Liverpool 8.

We would take turns pushing him in his little pushchair. Of course, we still got into the odd scrape but nothing too serious. Once I remember passing the coal yard coming back from Ninny Lizzy's and there was a hole in the fence with coal coming out of it. Free coal, we thought, a gift from God. What did we do? We piled all the coal we could into the pram with Ian still in it. Every square inch of the pram was full and we piled it so high around Ian that all you could see was his little head poking out with his black hands resting on top. Ian thought it was great fun; he was the centre of attention and even grabbed a piece of coal to see what it tasted like.

He was black as the hobs of hell, but we thought Mum and Dad would be so happy with all the free coal we'd brought home for the family. A little carbolic soap and Ian would be as good as new. Of course, Mum and Dad didn't see it that way and, although Dad offloaded every piece of coal and seemed quite pleased, Mum ranted like a madwoman and I was convinced we'd brought the nerves on again.

We were barred from taking Ian out for a few days but, once he started getting under Mum's feet again, she relented, although we were given a stern lecture about what we could and couldn't do with him.

One day as we left with Ian, Mum issued a final warning: 'Don't be going taking him to them bloody empty houses. D'ya hear me?'

Brian and I looked at each other. Had she known we'd been in those derelict houses?

At the broken back lane gate outside one of Crown Street's empty houses, the two of us argued over whether or not we could take Ian in.

'He'll cry if we don't take him in,' said Brian. 'We always take him in.'

'But Mum said we couldn't,' I countered.

'But she won't know.'

'She will.'

'She won't.'

'She will. Mums always find out, that's what mums do best.'

'Don't be daft,' he insisted. 'She's at home.'

Brian was right but I was having none of it. Mum's words were still fresh in my mind and her handprints still on me arse. Although I couldn't hear her voice, it was as if she would somehow know by magical telepathy if we took him into those empty houses. I was convinced of it.

Just then we had a great idea. Ian loved cowboys and Indians so we told him we were starting a game. I told him he was a cowboy and that he had been captured by the Indians (Brian and me). We played out the game and lifted him out of his pushchair whooping and wailing like red Indians. We stood either side and frogmarched him to the nearest lamp post where we tied him to it with his snake belt.

We told him he would need to wait until we came back.

'Where are you goin'?' he said.

We looked at him as if he was stupid. 'To get more cowboys, of course.'

'Aahhh.' He nodded, glad to be playing such an important part in the game.

What a brilliant plan, Brian and me could change the game to *Wuthering Heights* and Ian was safe as houses because he couldn't go anywhere. Fantastic… almost foolproof. Almost…

How could we have known that Mum had gone out for some bread and milk? She found Ian tied to the lamp post screaming his eyes out and she came looking for us. When she found us in the empty derelict houses, she ragged us both all the way home. I swear Ian suffered a bigger trauma the way Mum shouted and bawled all the way back home than he ever did getting tied to a lamp post for an hour... or was it longer? We weren't allowed out for a week, no matter how much we begged and cried. She kept us in even on Saturday when Dad's horses were running.

Ian grew up with a stammer, but I swear it was nothing we did to him, honest. He stammered long before we left him tied to that bloody lamp post. The other kids took the mickey out of him a little bit but Brian and me would always stick up for him and Mum said he would grow out of it. I wish he'd grown out of it before Mrs Gee's dog got a hold of him though.

Mrs Gee lived on the first landing in the corner tenements at the end of our street and had a big Alsatian dog called Major. It wasn't vicious, just as mad as a box of frogs. Mrs Gee explained to us that it would never bite or chase us if we called out his name loudly as it would think we were its friends. Sure enough, as soon as Mrs Gee called out 'Major', that dog would immediately sit, and turn from a big grizzly bear into an obedient little poodle. Then it would wag its tail waiting for her next command.

Major escaped every now and again and, if it saw any kids, a chase would start. It would tear after you but no one ever worried because if you couldn't shin up a wall or a fence you could just shout its name. At the sound of 'Major, no! Major, no!', the dog would come to a halt wagging its tail as if by magic. But, if you didn't include the magic word 'Major', it would bite you.

Once, when Ian was about four years old, Brian, Ian and I had gone to Ali's shop on the corner for sweets. As we passed Mrs Gee's tenement block, Major was cocking his leg against a lamp post. As soon as the dog saw us, it raced towards us, so we turned and legged it towards the wall of one of the ground-floor flats so we could jump up to get out the way. Me and Brian managed to escape, but inevitably, Ian couldn't run so fast, and Major was catching up with him.

'Just shout Major!' we screamed at Ian.

Hearing the sound of its own name, the dog stopped, but had second thoughts when it realised the cry hadn't come from Ian. So it started chasing him again.

We tried again. 'Major!' we shouted at Ian. 'Shout Major!'

This time, Ian turned to face the dog, ready to call out its name. But of course he couldn't.

'M...M...M...M...'

That bloody stutter.

'Shout Major,' I squealed.

'Major,' shouted Brian.

'Fuckin' Major! Shout, "Get down, Major."'

'M...M...M...'

Too late. By now, that brute of a bloody dog had sunk its teeth into Ian's arm and dragged him to the ground. Ian was still screaming but couldn't scream the name of his attacker, so we shouted the magic word once again. Fortunately, this time, as soon as the dog heard its name, it sat down smiling and began to wag its tail as Ian continued to writhe on the deck in agony. I swear the dog looked at him as if to say, 'What's up with him?' Major had done little more than broken Ian's skin, but he still needed to go to hospital where they put two small stitches into his arm.

Ian's stutter was another source of worry to Mum. No

wonder her nerves were bad, we must have driven her crackers. I had a voice like a foghorn, Brian twitched and tapped his leg every five minutes, and then there was Ian's stutter. She must have thought she'd given birth to The Three Stooges.

Then there was the day all three of us got a letter home from school. No other kids in my class got one. In fact, there were only four in the whole school who did. As I walked home with Brian and Ian, I tried to convince us all that it was because we'd been really good. But at what?

We all stood in the lounge grinning as Mum opened the letters one by one, taking in the contents before moving on to the next one. Her face was a picture of study; she was obviously thinking about our reward.

'Have we been good at school, Mum?' I asked.

'Yeah,' she said.

'What have we been good at?'

'Catching.'

'Catching?'

'Catchin' bloody nits, that's what. Now get in that friggin' bath, you dirty buggers.'

The tin bath normally reserved for a Sunday night was pulled out and placed in front of the fire and it was filled with water much too hot for our little bodies. Mum scrubbed – literally scrubbed – and then Dad rubbed us down with a towel rougher than sandpaper as we stood on a copy of the *Liverpool Echo* to catch the drips and nits. Nan, who was half blind, was up next in line with a bottle of vinegar in her hand and dragged the nit comb through our hair taking half of our scalp with it. Nan said that the vinegar would burst the eggs. I swear our heads would nearly be bleeding and it felt as if the comb had no teeth in it. By the end of the operation, we were all screaming in pain but were comforted when the nit patrol decided to give us a big doorstep jam butty to take our minds off the pain.

I have happy memories of the long summer holidays and of the winter too even though it was bitterly cold in the tenements in the days before central heating. In the winter, Nan always made us wear liberty bodices. They were a type of combination vest and knickers that had rubber buttons all the way up the front. We were then trussed up in jumpers that had more holes than the ozone layer, with a scarf wrapped around our neck and chest, tied in a knot on our back. Next, black wellington boots, a duffle coat and a balaclava with a pair of mitts on a piece of string which were fed up each sleeve in order that they wouldn't get lost. (Don't ask me. I can't figure that one out either.) I remember Ian's string being a little too short and as he went for a piece of snow with his right hand his left hand took on an involuntary action of its own.

Like all kids we loved the snow and dreaded when it turned into that awful slush, though it still didn't stop us from chucking slush balls. Brian, Ian and me would go off like three little Scotts of the Antarctic to play in the snow for hours then head for home bloody freezing, our toes throbbing and our legs ripped to bits with welly rash. All three of us would jostle for position trying to hog the roaring fire to get warm, until our skin turned bright red and Nan would be saying, 'Don't be standing too close to the bloody fire. You'll get corned-beef legs.'

I try my hardest to keep the good memories of those days at the front of my mind and I love talking about them and laughing with anyone who cares to listen, especially my brothers. While some memories are hard to talk about, let alone write, I prefer to think of happy times: Christmas, Hallowe'en and Bonfire Night.

Bonfire Night itself was great, although we never had any fireworks, just sparklers. We'd beg Dad to let us set them off but he'd make us wait until we'd finished our tea, by which time it was really dark. Even Ian was allowed to hold the odd one under the close supervision of Dad.

The run-up to Guy Fawkes' night was just as great. We'd dress our Ian up as a Guy, standing outside Ali's sweet shop taking pennies from anyone who passed, and trying to convince people that we'd made him. There'd be plenty of wood for us to collect too, but it had to be protected from rival gangs who lived in the nearby tenement blocks at Myrtle House. Everyone would be trying to steal each other's wood to see who could build the biggest bonnie in the area. Sometimes it was an all-out war, with the bigger lads throwing stones and kicking lumps out of each other for the sake of a plank of wood or an old settee. We'd watch in admiration as they turned the old wood, chairs and orange boxes into a huge wigwam towering into the sky. How we waited until 5 November before we set it alight, I'll never know.

Every back lane, every street and every tenement seemed to have a bonfire. Health and safety didn't come into it in those days and the glow in the pitch-black sky in Liverpool 8 on Bonfire Night could be seen for miles around. We'd throw potatoes on the glowing embers as the fire died down and sit as close as we dared, looking up into the night sky for the fireworks that were being set off around the city. It made me think that heaven was having a huge party.

About, about, in reel and rout
The death fires danced at night;
The water like witches oils,
Burnt green, and blue, and white.

Every day was like a party. Even though we had nothing, somehow our parents seemed to be able to provide just enough to make these special days a joy. They struggled and no doubt did without other things. I will forever be in their debt, God love them both.

Christmas was different because everyone knew that Santa Claus provided all your presents, though I couldn't quite understand how some kids got more than others. You'd think the fat get would have been able to even it out a little better, wouldn't you?

Our Christmases were not fancy – they were basic, with only one or two little presents and a bag or two of sweets each – but to us they were special and not once did we ever wake up disappointed. Every year, Mum would take us on a trip to TJ Hughes' store on London Road, where we'd watch the dancing waters in the grotto absolutely mesmerised as they danced a tune to the music. They were something else. Once the show was over, off we'd go to see Santa in the grotto, excitedly knowing that in a few short days he'd be coming down our chimney. A couple of days later, the Christmas parades with all the floats would heave and groan their way through the town centre. Sometimes I wish those events had been frozen in time, just like our fingers and toes were in the snow. It was great to be a kid back then; I wished we could have stayed that age forever.

It was at Christmas 1966, when I was eight years old, that Santa was particularly generous. I remember it well because we all got a World Cup Willie mascot to celebrate the fact that England had won the World Cup that summer. Dad had been knocked over by a wagon some months earlier when he was delivering his parcels for the railway. Thankfully, he wasn't hurt too badly but was awarded £100 compensation in the middle of

December. I swear he spent every penny of his compensation on that Christmas.

Mum could hardly contain herself; she had woken us at five in the morning to show us how good Father Christmas had been. She was wide awake and grinning as she woke three bleary-eyed youngsters from their slumber and forced us out of bed. So that year, we got loads of presents. We started with the pillowcases by the bottom of the bed: cars, a Snakes and Ladders board game, Tiddlywinks and a climb-in *Dr Who* Dalek for Ian. In the living room, there were two dolls for me – a Tiny Tears and a Tressy – and in the middle of the room was a brand-new Chopper bike for Brian. There was a police car with a siren, a Spirograph, Ker-Plunk...

Santa had even brought Mum a pair of new curtains. She said it was the first thing she had ever had that wasn't on tick. We found out later they were magic curtains that wouldn't go on fire. But we found out by accident.

One night, Brian and me were in on our own watching telly. The telly was from Radio Rentals and had to be fed with a sixpence via a slot in the back. That sixpence would last four or five hours, but it was so annoying when it would run out – especially if we were watching something good and you had to crawl around the back and insert another tanner. The set was so close to the wall it was difficult to see the slot but Brian, being smaller than me, could crawl under the legs of the television to insert the money. To give him enough light to see, I'd get some newspaper and light it from the fire. But that night, when I lit the newspaper and ran towards the telly, the whole bloody sheet of newspaper seemed to have caught fire. I panicked, and the sheet landed on the floor beside the bottom of the curtains. Brian jumped up and down on the flames to put them out like he was Michael Flatley. Yet the curtains never caught fire. They never had a mark on them, not even a singe... They were magic...

What a great opportunity to make a little extra cash, we thought, so we would bring our mates in to see the 'magic curtains' and put a match to them. The kids stood back in amazement as the curtains held firm and never caught fire no matter how many matches we held underneath them. We charged a penny a time for the kids to try to set them on fire, even offering a refund if they succeeded. And we thought Mrs Gee's dog was as mad as a box of frogs!

However, our new business venture was put to bed early when Mum came home one day and caught us red-handed. Picture the scene as she walked into the room to find half a dozen raggy-arsed kids trying to set her bloody house on fire. We had red hands and red arses when my dad got home from his shift at work.

CHAPTER THREE

GRANDDAD

I fear thee, Ancient Mariner!
I fear thy skinny hand!
And thou art long, and lank, and brown
As the ribb'd sea sand.

But now I must force myself to discuss darker days.
The dark days are locked in a black closet deep inside my head, and that's where I'd prefer to leave them. Granddad is in that dark place and his whole story needs to be told in the pages of this book, as it may help others who have suffered in a similar way. It has been so hard for me to gather my thoughts on this subject. Scotty has been insistent that I tell this story, but also very understanding. He suggested that using a tape-recorder might help with recapturing difficult memories. Sitting with the tape-recording machine with my hand shaking, I try to press the 'record' button, but I know that, once I do that, I must relive those awful memories again. Even if I complete the exercise, would it be as easy to erase those memories from my mind as it would be to erase my voice from the tape?

Incredibly, I succeed; after several days, the tapes are finished. Scotty comes over to listen, but I need to leave the room while he does. I hide in the kitchen for what seems like forever and I hear the tape click stop. When I come back through to the lounge, he has a face as white as a ghost's and there are tears brimming in his eyes. I have a thousand different emotions coursing through my veins. When he leaves, I have to erase the tapes immediately.

I haven't mentioned Granddad much up to now, as, to be quite honest, he didn't figure in my life an awful lot in the early years. Then, he was just a normal, loving granddad. By the time I was eight he was retired, but I can't remember him being in the house that often. He didn't have the time of day for our dad and made his feelings well known, which was a mystery to me. Dad was a good husband and a good dad, never out of work and he always put the family before the pub, unlike a lot of men in those days who would drink away the majority of their wages in the bars and working men's clubs in Liverpool 8. Yet, whenever Dad came into the house, Granddad would make a point of getting up out of his chair and leaving, muttering something under his breath. It must have been hard enough for Dad to be sharing his house with his wife's parents under those circumstances. Dad was a very placid man but I remember huge rows between him and Granddad, with Mum and Nan trying to keep the peace.

If there were too many people at home, Granddad would disappear. We could be playing together as kids with Mum, and he would seem quite happy, but then Nan would come in and he would announce he was off out to the pub or for a walk along the Pier Head. Occasionally, he would take Brian and me with him; occasionally Ian would come too in his pushchair.

At the Pier Head, we'd gaze down the river looking out to sea, and we'd hear one of Granddad's vivid stories. He had been a merchant seaman when he was a young man and obviously missed his life at sea. He spent long periods away from home; perhaps that's why I don't remember him. Maybe that's why he couldn't handle retirement too well – confined to a small two-bed tenement, with a wife, his daughter and her husband and family – when he'd been used to vast expanses of water and space as far as the eye could see.

Looking out from the Pier Head, Granddad would tell us tales about his ships and his journeys to India and Africa, and how long the ships would take to get there. He'd tell us all about the cargoes his ships were delivering, as well as the weird food and spices he would bring back into the Mersey. He'd name every ship he ever worked on, and tell us how wonderful they were, how many were built on the Mersey, and how the Liverpool shipbuilders and dockers were the best in the whole wide world. Then he'd tell us the not-so-nice stories: freak waves, storms and shipwrecks, and a huge big bird called an albatross that spelled doom for any sailor who ever harmed one.

And then he'd recite a poem by Coleridge called *The Rime of the Ancient Mariner*, in which the mariner was the navigator, advising all the sailors which way to go. We'd hear about how those poor sailors were stuck near the Equator in a place called the Doldrums. The Doldrums was a notorious area for sailors because a deadly calm could trap sailing ships for days or weeks on end as they waited for enough wind to power their sails. The sailors in Coleridge's poem had run out of food and essential supplies.

> *Water, water, everywhere,*
> *Nor any drop to drink.*

You could imagine that God would send all the bad sailors to the Doldrums. I'd ask Granddad if he'd ever been there, and he'd nod his head and tell me how his ship had survived.

> *Day after day, day after day,*
> *We stuck, nor breath nor motion;*
> *As idle as a painted ship*
> *Upon a painted ocean.*

Granddad told us how the sailors got stuck in the Doldrums and blamed the Mariner for their thirst. The crew of the ship turned on their navigator and forced the Mariner to wear a dead albatross around his neck as a punishment.

> *…What evil looks*
> *Had I from old and young!*
> *Instead of the cross, the Albatross*
> *About my neck was hung.*

That floundering ship stayed in the Doldrums until its sailors came across some sort of ghost ship, which placed a curse on the sailors as a punishment for killing the albatross. One by one the sailors all died. I imagined my granddad as the poem's sole survivor – the Ancient Mariner himself.

And we'd walk back home, Brian and me asking the same questions over and over again about that strange bird called Albert Ross. Granddad answered all our questions, listened and laughed and cuddled us into him to keep warm if it was cold and wet, while we made the long journey home on the top deck of the 86 bus. And back home he'd help us off with our coats and hats and scarves and those bloody mitts on a string, and stand us in front of the fire to get warm.

GRANDDAD

Coleridge's poem was beautiful, so descriptive and yet somehow scary. I can remember those lines which were repeated so often by my granddad. Yet I can't remember my granddad's voice. I can remember his facial expressions, the clothes he wore on the Pier Head to protect himself from the howling winds that whistled up the Mersey but I can't remember his bloody voice. Why? I remember the neighbours' voices and even the ragman's when he shouted, 'Any ol' rags,' and the voice of every single member of my family long since gone. But not Granddad's.

I want to remember Granddad's voice. I want to remember the good times with my granddad… only the good times.

I loved our granddad. I loved him when he took a big cooking apple, sliced the top off, hollowed out the core and replaced it with sugar. He'd then replace the top and call it the apple hat. At 11D Windsor Gardens, we had a small black oven next to the fire and Granddad would bake the apple for 20 minutes, making us wait patiently, then take it out, slice it in half and give it to me and Brian while he looked on smiling.

I've already explained that Dad and Granddad didn't get on. How Dad managed those years living in that house I'll never know, but events inevitably came to a head in the form of a huge fight. It woke me from a deep sleep and I heard Granddad and Dad cursing and swearing at each other through the bedroom wall. I could make out Mum crying and Nan trying in vain to keep the peace. I wandered through to see what was going on but Nan ushered me back to bed in that soft soothing voice of hers. She was like an oasis in a desert in the highly charged atmosphere of the living room.

I lay awake and prayed to God it would stop.

It didn't.

The argument went on and on and eventually someone

33

stormed out of the house nearly taking the door off the hinges. The whole house seemed to shake.

A couple of weeks later, at the beginning of 1968, we were on the move. Not far away – we were still in the Windsor Gardens tenement block, but this time at 3C. We were one flight of stairs down from Nan and Granddad, with no more than a three-minute walk between both front doors. It probably wasn't far enough for Dad but at last he was free from Granddad. Mum and Dad spent every last penny they had furnishing the house and I remember friends and other members of the family turning up at the house with old sofas, scraps of carpets, rugs and pieces of crockery that had more chips in them than the local fish shop. It didn't matter; this was great, we were getting our own house and, to me and my brothers, it was one big adventure, a new beginning.

Brian and Ian were shown their very own room and I still remember the look of joy on their little faces. But where was I going to sleep? I asked Mum, who was busy unpacking a cardboard box with baby stuff, as – unbeknown to us – she was pregnant with our new little brother.

'You just stay where you are, Christine,' she said without looking up. 'You look after your nan.'

That was it. No more discussions. But I was happy enough. I may not have had my own room like my brothers did, but then again I couldn't imagine going to sleep without snuggling up to Nan.

So I had the best of both worlds: two houses I could flit between whenever the fancy took me. I had an odd night sleeping with Mum and Dad at 3C but kept my favourite spot in Nan's bed.

On Christmas Day 1968, my young brother David was born at 3C Windsor Gardens. He was named after Mum's favourite

Christmas carol, 'Once In Royal David's City'. David was the opposite of Ian. He was tiny and didn't seem to grow much. Even when he was three, he only looked like he was about a year old. We used to torment the life out of him, the poor bugger, and he would throw himself on the floor holding his breath till he went blue in the face. It used to frighten the shit out of our mum.

We were one big, mad, but happy family. Or so it seemed to anyone looking in.

When I think of Granddad, I think of two people, two faces, two different men, a gentle old man and Coleridge's 'Ancient Mariner'. I feel many things – fear, betrayal, anger, bitterness, disgust, even guilt – but above all I feel confusion. I want to hate him but I can't. I love him like a granddad and when he died I cried for days.

I've talked with Scotty long and hard on which way to approach these difficult next few chapters so that I may feel comfortable with it, but I know that I will never feel comfortable with it. I wish life was like a big blackboard where a big chalky blackboard rubber could wipe those memories away, so they would disappear in the dust.

It was back before the rest of the family moved out of 11D, that Granddad changed. Not overnight, it was a gradual change, but a definite change even so. One minute he would be telling us a story as Nan looked on smiling and, within half an hour of her going out, he would take on a totally different character. Our granddad changed from Dr Jekyll into Mr Hyde.

What I'm about to tell you continues to haunt me through nightmares that show no signs of stopping. In these nightmares, I am Christine Murray aged eight. The memories are clear, vivid and painful, and still torment me to this day.

'Please stop, Granddad, stop picking on Brian. He 'asn't done not'n.'

'Christine, help me, help me, please.'

Granddad is picking me little brother up by the throat and holding him up in the air like a ballerina doll. His feet are off the floor and our Brian is struggling to breathe.

'Stop, Granddad, please stop.'

I pull at me granddad's trouser leg and he lashes out with his leg. I bounce into the corner of the room and now I am crying.

I can't look. I cover my face with my hands as I hear the most horrible choking and gurgling sounds, and I know me little brother is in bother.

I hear the clock ticking loudly through all the noise. I know from me teacher at school that each tick is a second, and as I count – one, two, three, four, five, six – still Brian is choking. I don't want to look but I have to. I have to do something. Brian is looking at me, his eyes begging me to help.

Tick… tick… tick… tick.

'Please, Granddad,' I shout but he is not listening. I shout again, this time louder and I am crying.

'Leave 'im, leave 'im.'

This isn't me granddad, not the same lovely granddad that takes us to the pier and tells us them lovely stories.

'Please, God, stop him, please. God, tell him to stop. Help, please, God, please, God, please, God, tell him to get off our Brian.'

Me hands are clasped tight together.

God never answers me prayers. Where are you, God? You're supposed to be everywhere; come to Windsor Gardens, it's number 11D.

'Please, God, please, God.'

I'm praying harder than I have ever prayed before.

'11D, God… 11D Windsor Gardens, Liverpool 8.'

And then it's over and Granddad lets Brian drop to the floor.

'Thank you, God,' I whisper as I rush over to Brian and Granddad walks away. Poor Brian, he wants to cry but can't cry 'cause he can hardly breathe. I drape my body over him and cuddle him. I can't do no more. I want to do more but I can't think of not'n.

'Sorry, Brian, I'm sorry, so sorry.'

Granddad calls it the choking game.

* * *

The following week, Granddad plays the choking game again and I have the same feelings of desperation and hopelessness.

God was too slow last time, so this time I'm crying out for me mum.

Granddad warns me that the more I cry, the longer he chokes me little brother. Brian is looking at me again from the corner of his eyes as they are bustin' from his skull. I look into those beautiful blue eyes, and see the panic and terror. And then it's over and he sits sobbing in me arms, all the while asking me, 'Why didn't you stop him, Christine?'

His snots are falling between his trembling lips and, although I cuddle him, I make sure I don't touch the snots.

'Don't let him do it again, Christine… please.'

Oh, Brian, my brother, my hero, my friend. He made me a cart of wood and pushed me up and down Crown Street making me feel like a queen. He played Tarzan and Jane with me – when we would jump from the top of our mum's wardrobe on to the bed, pretending that the bed was an alligator-infested lagoon and that the coats on the bed were the alligators to be fought off. He'd huddle with me underneath coats praying that the dark days of abuse and torment would vanish and the good days would remain.

* * *

Nan has the cataracts. She is blind as a bat, me mum says, and she needs to go into hospital. So I have to look after me granddad, she tells me.

'I don't want to look after him,' I explain.

'Why not?' Mum asks. 'He's your granddad.'

I want to tell her he isn't like me granddad any more but I'm thinking what he told me would happen to me and our Brian if we told anyone. He said we'd go into the naughty home and Mum and Dad wouldn't ever come to see us. We'd be pushed on a ferry down the Mersey and never seen again.

'What's cat 'n axe?' Brian asks innocently. He's a bit thick, me brother, fancy not knowin' that the cataracts are bad eyes.

'Nan's going to hospital for an operation to get new eyes,' I tell him.

'She's getting new eyes?'

'Yes.'

'What, two new eyes?'

I look at me mum and she smiles and nods.

'Two new ones,' I reply confidently.

'Will they be glass like me ollies?' (Ollies was the name we had for marbles.)

'Stupid div,' I say. 'No, they're real ones. She'll get two new 'uns.'

'I bet that hurts,' says Brian.

Me mum and me are getting Nan ready for the hospital and she is a little strange. Quiet like. Me mum says she is nervous but at least when she comes out she'll be able to see further than the other side of the living room.

GRANDDAD

I'm not sleeping with Nan tonight. I'm gonna miss snugglin' up to her. Perhaps Granddad will keep me warm. He hasn't played the choking game for a while. Maybe he's back to our normal granddad.

I'm sleeping when Granddad comes to bed but he wakes me up moaning and groaning.

'What's wrong, Granddad?'

He turns over.

'Me stomach, Christine. It hurts terrible. It needs rubbed.'

Granddad reaches under the covers for me hand.

'Will you rub me belly, Christine? Make Granddad all better.'

Granddad puts me hand on his stomach and makes me start rubbing him. I pull me hand away straight away and he clouts me on the back of me head.

'Rub me belly.'

He puts me hand down there again.

'I don't like it.'

'Rub me belly. You want Granddad to get better, don't you?'

Before I can answer, he hits me again.

He closes me hand round his belly and makes me rub it faster. It doesn't feel right, all lumpy and hard. I tell him he needs to go to the hospital like me nan and they'll give him a new belly like they're giving me nan new eyes. Perhaps Granddad will get a bed next to Nan.

He doesn't answer; he is moaning in pain. His hand is clasped around my hand squeezing me hard and we are both rubbing at his sore belly.

He seems to relax and suddenly his moaning and groaning has stopped. I think I have made it better. He will be pleased and maybe won't make us play the choking game again.

In the morning, he orders me into a big bath he has filled. Now, after I have made his belly all better, he's being nasty to me.

'How's your belly, Granddad?'

At first, he doesn't answer me. Then he tells me I am dirty and filthy and disgusting. He grabs me by the neck and says if I tell anyone what happened to his belly they'll take me away forever and everyone will hate me and I won't see Brian for 50 years.

I'm crying in the bath telling Granddad that I'm sorry I didn't fix his belly. He's throwing cups of water into my face so I can hardly breathe.

'I'm sorry, Granddad, I won't tell anyone. I'm sorry.'

'Shut the fuck up, you snivelling get.'

My other granddad never uses the fuck word, never ever, ever.

And still he throws the water in my face and uses the fuck word again and others I haven't heard before and grabs me by the hair and forces my head under the water and I can't breathe. Eventually, he lets me up and I gulp in the air as quick as I can so I don't die.

And then he shouts, 'Now get out of that bath and get dried.'

I lie in the bath crying until the water is freezing cold. I am so scared and want to ask Granddad what I have done that is so bad. I thought I was helping him. Perhaps he is right, I am filthy and disgusting.

I sob out loud, 'Don't make me go away, Granddad, please. I love Brian, Brian needs me to protect him, please, Granddad, no... I won't ever, ever, ever tell anyone, honest to God, I won't ever tell.'

Me mum finds me shivering in the bath but tells me to hurry up as we have to visit Nan in the hospital. She asks me where Granddad is and I tell her I don't know.

We aren't allowed in hospital to see Nan. The hospital won't allow me and Brian in, only me mum. So we are standing by the wall across the road from the hospital and Mum says she will

GRANDDAD

get Nan to wave out of her window at the end of the ward. Dad isn't with us, he's working, but Granddad hasn't come either, which doesn't seem right to me.

I ask Brian what he thinks but he calls Granddad a bastard and says he doesn't care. I scold him and tell him not to use words like that about our granddad. Brian and me look up at the big hospital, and to floor number seven. Mum has told us that, if we look there, she will get Nan out of bed and make her wave to us. Five minutes after Mum goes into the hospital, we see people at the place where she pointed.

The tiny figures are hard to see but there are two of them and they are waving, and me and Brian wave back and... yes... it's me mum and Nan. I'm glad I've walked right across Liverpool to see her. I hope she comes back to 11D Windsor Gardens soon.

***

Nan returned from hospital with much-improved eyesight, and I can remember cuddling her tight all night the first night she was home. I hugged her so tightly she said she could hardly breathe. But I knew I would be safe now. Nan, my protector, was back home.

CHAPTER FOUR

DOWN WITH SCHOOL

Her lips were red, her looks were free,
Her locks were yellow as gold:
Her skin was as white as leprosy,
The nightmare Life-in-Death was she,
Who thicks man's blood with cold.

Primary school for us was St Saviour's on Crown Street. There's a hospital there now. All of us went to St Saviour's, even my dad had been there.

I won't use my class teacher's real name but will call him Mr Smith. He had the bushiest eyebrows I'd ever seen, and the biggest, loudest voice I'd ever heard. It was in this voice that he told us we were thick – especially me, or so it seemed. You'd answer one thing wrong and that was it.

'Murray, I can't believe how thick you are. You are as thick as a brick.'

And, of course, all the other kids would laugh. Day after day, week after week, every single term, I was told I was thick and eventually I started to believe it. I began to wonder what the use was of trying to learn anything. It was the same story back home; when no one else was in, Granddad would be saying how disgusting I was, and how the bad things that happened were always my fault. And then at school, Mr Smith would tell me the class's bad results were all my fault. The verbal assault from both of them damaged me right through to adulthood. Teachers reading this, please take note.

So I made a stand: I rebelled and decided Mr Smith was going to teach me nothing. I became abusive to him and cheeky, and even when he asked me questions that I knew the right answer to I would give him the wrong answers deliberately.

He would say, 'You are as thick as two short planks, Murray.' Yet I knew that Mr Smith was frustrated, angry that his teaching skills were being put to the test, and wondering if he was going wrong somewhere. It became a constant battle, a war that was talked about in the playground and no doubt in the staffroom.

One day, we got a rare treat and watched a film in class about the Sahara Desert. It was a relief to get a break from Mr Smith's monotone voice. We sat and watched the film in silence learning about how deserts were created, how the sands moved and expanded over time, and about the creatures that survived in the hostile environment, how cold it was at night, and how hot it was during the day. It was so effective that I wished every lesson could be like that.

But, when it finished, Mr Smith spoiled it.

'Right, Murray,' he shouted, 'what was the name of the film we have just watched?'

(That's how Mr Smith spoke to us, always by our last name.)

What a stupid question, I thought. Ask something about the desert or erosion or a camel even. But the name of the film?

'I don't know, sir,' I replied.

'You don't know what you've just sat and watched for the last hour, you stupid girl?'

All the other kids in the class were laughing and I loathed him with all my heart.

He pointed at the screen. 'Look at the screen; it's there in big letters, you imbecile.'

I shook my head. I could see the words up on the screen but couldn't make sense of them. This is why the children were laughing, they could read, but my mind was frozen and I couldn't.

The laughter continued as Mr Smith walked over to me. He looked around at the class and smiled, revelling in his comedy act. He pointed at his temple, tapped it two or three times, grinned, then looked at me and pointed. My classmates laughed louder. The bastard knew I couldn't read but still he persisted in humiliating me.

Mr Smith was in my face by now and I could smell his stale breath as he roared at me. 'I confess I never really knew just how thick you were, Murray. I'll ask you again, what was the name of the bloody film?'

He waited for an answer that never came, then he pointed back to the screen. 'It's there in black and white, you idiot!'

I could feel my face going red. I wanted to read the words, honestly I did, but they were making no sense; all the letters were mixed up. I could feel the tears of shame welling up in my eyes, my face flushed red.

This time Mr Smith really shouted. 'Tell me what the name of the film is, Murray... NOW!'

I stood up and used the words Granddad used. 'It's your fuckin' film, you should fuckin' know what it's fuckin' called.'

The kids weren't laughing now. Those words had never been uttered in Mr Smith's classroom before, and I was quite pleased at the effect they had on both the class and the teacher, whose chin all but hit the desk.

'What did you say, girl?'

'You fuckin' heard, it's your fuckin' film, you tell me the

name of it.' I pointed to the screen. 'It's right there in fuckin' black and fuckin' white.'

Mr Smith launched himself at me and grabbed me by my arm, pulling me from behind the desk.

'Get off, you dickhead.'

'Get out of my class, you filthmonger,' he roared.

I pulled back from him. 'Get off me. Don't be grabbing me because you don't know what your own fuckin' film is called.'

Mr Smith was bursting at the gills, beetroot red with anger. He almost threw me through the classroom door, and frogmarched me to the head teacher. Mr Mcloughlin was a lovely man, and he asked me what I had done softly and sensitively. I hung my head as he asked me to think again about my actions. Mr Mcloughlin had taught my dad and he told me how disappointed he would be, but, when I left his office, he asked me to pass on his regards to Dad. How nice was that? Of all the teachers at that school, I only have fond memories and respect for Mr Mcloughlin.

Mr Smith, though, was not satisfied. He stood and fumed. He recorded the incident in a punishment book and then dragged me back to the classroom by my ear. He made me stand in the corridor and told me he would be back with the cane. After the bastard had made me wait at least 20 minutes for my punishment, he raised the cane high above his head. I watched him do that, then squeezed my eyes shut and gritted my teeth waiting for the contact.

He hit me across the right hand six times with that stick. On the fifth blow, I broke down and burst into tears. It felt like my hand had been stung by a million wasps. He smiled as he broke me, then delivered the sixth stroke with such power I swear he nearly broke my wrist. It was a big victory for him in our ongoing war.

'Not so cocky now, are you, Murray?' He smirked as he walked away.

I spent more time outside Mr Smith's class than I did in it. Sometimes, after 20 or 30 minutes he would shout out my name for no reason.

'Murray... outside now.'

'What for, sir? I ain't done not'n.'

'No, but you will soon. Now get out.'

So I'd have no choice but to leave the class or another visit to the head would result.

Inevitably, I hated school. Mr Smith was definitely the worst of the teachers, but most of the others were little better. If you couldn't keep up or got a question wrong, they would rap a ruler across the back of your knuckles and think it was such a hoot. The rest of the class would crack up laughing, just thankful that it wasn't them.

Nothing from lessons seemed to sink in with me. At times I wanted to learn, I really did, but then my spirit would be broken by an abusive teacher with a strap or a ruler, and I would just think to myself, 'Fuck them... fuck them all.'

In any case, my head was full of different things. I had enough problems to worry about at home. For one thing, Mum was still not well. Nan would help me get ready for school, walk me up to 3C to collect Brian and Ian, who'd still be in bed, while Mum would rock backwards and forwards in her dressing gown on the sofa. She would whisper gently that we didn't have to go to school today and smile and stare at the walls. I'd be quite happy and put a little breakfast together for Brian and Ian, then take them out of Mum's way while she nursed my youngest brother, David.

This routine worked fine, and I'd get Mum to write a little note for the school saying that she'd been ill through the night and had overslept. It seemed quite easy at the time and of course I didn't have to suffer the humiliation at the hands of certain so-called teachers who couldn't teach a dog to bark.

Occasionally, the school board would turn up at the house. If that happened, either Nan would help us to get to school for a few weeks or Mum would rally herself. That worked for Ian and Brian, but by now I'd had enough of being abused at school as well as at home and at the first opportunity I would be off out the school gates.

Poor Mum couldn't cope at all. Thank the Lord for our nan who did what she could. She set us chores to help Mum who at times could barely drag herself out of bed. Before long, Brian and I were doing most of the housework. We did most things for our mum, like cleaning up and washing – which we were quite happy to do – but inevitably there was the odd argument.

Early one morning, Brian and I were in the kitchen arguing about whose turn it was to wash up. We were shouting at each other when Mum seemed to appear out of thin air. She casually took the bowl of dishes from the sink and chucked them through the window. Broken crockery and glass, splinters of wood, knives, forks and spoons sailed through the air as if in slow motion and crashed down into the street three storeys below. Panic-stricken, I looked out through the broken window convinced someone had been killed by our broken dishes. Thankfully, no one had been walking by.

'There,' she said. 'You don't have to argue now, our Brian and Christine, because there's no dishes.'

She smiled, turned and walked away again as silently as she'd appeared.

DOWN WITH SCHOOL

***

When no one is in the house Granddad still plays the choking game.

'Please stop, Granddad, please stop.'

CHAPTER FIVE

CONTROL

Each corse lay flat, lifeless and flat,
And, by the holy rood!
A man all light, a seraph-man
On every corse there stood.

Nan started feeling ill after having an earache that went on for weeks. I remember her standing by the fire then all of a sudden her hands would cover her ears. One day when it was really bad and the tears were welling up in her eyes Mum sent for the doctor, who came straight away. Within 20 minutes, he'd called an ambulance, and Nan was on her way to hospital. I'll never forget the sad look on Dr Sheiff's face as he stood with his big stethoscope round his neck. He'd known our nan many years, and it was as if he'd given up all hope.

I panicked. Suddenly, all the things that Granddad had threatened us with had come true. I loved my nan – in many ways I loved her just as much as my mum – and now it seemed she was being taken away from us.

When she had left and I was alone with Granddad, I swore to him that I hadn't told anyone about what had happened. He just shook his head and told me to be quiet. I was angry and disgusted with myself, but confused too, because, apart from Brian, I really hadn't told anyone.

⁎⁎

Nan has been discharged from hospital but I know she is not better and I am worried. She is visiting hospital quite a lot. There is something wrong with her throat and her voice too; she can hardly speak.

Sometimes she stays in overnight and I dread bedtimes. Granddad is still making me touch his Micky. I know it is not his belly now and I don't like it. Why do little girls have to do that to their granddads? It's not fair. Granddad is making me sleep close to him when Nan is away to keep him warm, he says. He wants me to keep his hands warm at nights and makes me wrap my legs round his hands and arms.

But then he touches me down there, on my 'Auntie Mary' and it doesn't feel nice and I know he shouldn't do that because our mum says you should never touch your 'Auntie Mary'. But then he tells me about the home for naughty boys and girls and calls me those horrible names again and again and makes me promise I won't tell anyone.

'I promise, Granddad, I promise.'

'Swear on your mum's life?'

'I swear, Granddad, I swear on me mum's life and Dad's and on baby Jesus's life too.'

'Swear on Nan's life?'

'Yes and me nan's as well.'

Nan looks awful. I hear Mum telling me dad she has the cancer disease and Mum is sobbing. I don't want her to go into hospital again. I like my house when Nan is there. Granddad tells me that it's all my fault and that Nan has caught the cancer because of those horrible things I do to him that I mustn't tell anyone about. He says if I tell anyone Nan will die and I will go to hell.

Not only that, but, when Nan goes to hospital, Granddad still plays the choking game. When he gets that look, and has Brian and me trapped in the living room, Brian starts crying even though Granddad hasn't said a word. It's the look.

'No, please, Granddad,' begs Brian as I try to stand between them. He never picks on me, always Brian. Please God let it be me. I know it will hurt but make it be me, God.

Granddad looks at me and smiles. It doesn't look like Granddad's smile, not like the smile on the Pier Head, or when he gives us cooking apples with sugar all the way through. It's not his smile. It's not my Granddad, it's someone else.

'Who wants to be first?'

Brian is on his knees, crying, shaking his head and begging. 'Please, no, Granddad.'

I don't want to play the game but I cannot stand watching me little brother suffer any longer.

'Me, I want to play the choking game.'

Granddad grins. 'Are you sure?'

Brian hasn't heard but can't believe his luck as Granddad bundles him out of the house and comes back to stand in front of me.

I am terrified as he comes towards me but I am feeling proud that I have saved and protected me little brother. He won't have to suffer.

I close my eyes tight like I did when I got the cane and wait for Granddad's hands to close around my throat. I tense my neck up and all I can hear is that ticking clock. Granddad winds that clock up every night. He has a little key that he keeps in his waistcoat pocket. No one can ever wind that clock up, only Granddad. Concentrate on the clock, I tell myself: tick... tick...

tick. The clock's on the mantle, strong, sturdy and safe. All of a sudden I am the clock and I am hiding inside; the clock is my heartbeat.

Nothing happens. There are no hands around my neck and I think that Granddad might have changed back to our nice granddad again.

I open my eyes. Granddad's trousers are round his ankles and his Micky is sticking out. He is touching his Micky and that's not right. Mum is always telling our Brian to stop fiddlin' with his Micky.

He steps forward with the look on his face again and reaches out and grabs a handful of my hair and forces my mouth open with his cold slimy fingers. Those fingers are not my granddad's; they are devil's fingers... devil's claws.

Brian finds me in a heap on the floor sobbing and this time it's him who comforts me, stroking my hair gently and wiping at the tears on my face.

'We'll take turns,' he says, trying to make me feel better about Granddad's game, but all I can hear is the ticking of the clock, as if someone has turned up the volume to a deafening volume. I feel as if my head is about to explode.

God forgive me.

* * *

Granddad controlled us both, and he degraded us. He told us it was a special secret that no one else could know about. They use the term 'grooming' these days, and that's what he did: he groomed us mentally, filled our heads with so much shit and lies and fear that we were too frightened and ashamed to breathe a single word of what was going on.

So the abuse just went on and on until there came a point where it felt normal. Then self-hatred came in, the self-loathing and, when I had a feeling of hating him, I felt like I was betraying him. I hated myself for hating him. Can you understand that?

God, I have to stop writing for a minute…

It's hard for me going back to those times. I don't want to relive them again and it still chokes me, just like a big plastic bag has been placed over my head and I can't breathe because I am suffocating. I am shaking with uncontrollable fear and agony of knowing that it happened. It makes no sense. For many a year, I have tried to come to terms with it, and tried to chase the nightmares away, but still they return all too regularly. I must fight hard to keep myself from going insane, forever chasing the demons of yesteryear away.

***

I haven't been to school again today. Mum said she is going out, taking David to the doctor's and I have to go round to help Nan. But Nan isn't home, only Granddad.

'No, Granddad, please.'

Granddad is forcing me on to the floor and lifting my dress up and I am bare down there and he can see my 'Auntie Mary'. I wish I had me knickers on but I only have one pair and they have been washed and are above the fireplace at me mum's.

'No, Granddad, please.'

This is not the choking game, but a new game. Granddad is so heavy and I can hardly breathe. I want to scream at him to stop; he is hurting me so much. I feel a hot pain like a red-hot poker; I am tearing down there, inside me. Me belly feels as if it is in me chest, me chest feels as if it is in me throat, and me throat is bursting through me eyeballs.

'No, Granddad,' I manage to blurt out. 'Play the choking

game, please play the choking game. Not this game, anything but this game.'

I don't like it. I don't like it. I want me granddad to get off. I don't want to play his game any more. I've asked Jesus to tell him I don't want to play, but he must've gone out because he's not listening, 'cause I must be bad and Jesus doesn't like bad people. I'm gonna tell Jesus's dad on him, because I'm not bad and he never comes to listen. He never listened either when the vicar asked him to make me sister Janet better. He didn't listen, he never listens.

I want Granddad to get off now. I close my eyes and focus on the clock, knowing that the end of my torment is controlled by its ticking. But then I remember that the clock's little winder is always kept in his trouser pocket. Granddad controls me and controls Brian, but he also controls that clock, and, even when my mind escapes into that clock on the mantle shelf, I haven't escaped... not really.

CHAPTER SIX

GOODBYE, NAN

Alone, alone, all, all alone,
Alone on a wide wide sea!
A never a saint took pity on
My soul in agony

My granddad had attacked me from the age of eight and continued to attack me and abuse me for four years. I tried to cope the best I could and live a normal life. As a child, I thought that every other little girl was going through the same thing. How would I have known otherwise? I couldn't talk about it because I was convinced if I breathed a word of what was happening I'd suffer a fate worse than death. I sincerely believed I would be sent away forever and never see Mum, Dad or my beautiful brothers ever again.

As a small girl, it doesn't get any worse than that, believe me. The fear of what would happen if the secret got out was worse than the abuse. All I could do was try to avoid being in the house on my own with my granddad and instead spent more and more time at my parents' house. I would only go to Granddad's during the day if I knew Nan was definitely home, but of course there were always times that I would find myself alone with him and he would abuse me.

I would go round at weekends and watch TV with Nan. I was always safe with Nan there, and she and Granddad would be sitting on the sofa and I'd sit beside Nan. It was such a nice comfortable scene, the three of us sitting there, and often I'd drift off and wonder if I'd dreamed up the abuse. Granddad would be fetching cups of tea for me and Nan and cracking funny jokes, and I'd think, 'How can he be so different, how can he act like that, knowing all he does about our special secrets?'

Only as an adult have I realised it was wrong, and become aware that many other children hadn't suffered as I had. Sometimes I look to excuse his behaviour, in order to punish myself. Did I sit on his knee too long, did I hug him too much? I can't hate him, because if I hate him I hate me. Hate is a horrible, horrible word and a horrible feeling to have inside you. Only if I forgive him can I forgive myself, and I do forgive him. And while you, my dear reader, might find that hard to believe, I mean it. I don't need a psychiatrist or a doctor to tell me how I feel because they'll never know how I feel, they'll never know the fear and terror and hurt I went through. I forgive him because that's how I get through it.

One night many years ago, I wrote everything down that had happened, everything. I sat there for hours and scribbled and scrawled as the tears fell on to the A4 sheets of paper. I filled about 10 pages: every feeling, silly things like what the weather was like at the time, the things he said, reactions and even the smells and noises I associated with certain events. And I took the pages out into the garden, then set fire to them in a metal bowl. I watched them go up in flames as the smoke billowed up into the night sky.

When the pages were nothing more than black ash, I threw those remains in the air. I didn't need that baggage living inside me rent free forever. There are days, as I've said, when those memories rise to the surface through my bad dreams, but I feel I can cope now because that baggage is not manifesting itself inside me; it's not eating away at me like a cancer, as it did when I was a young girl, a teenager and a young woman.

* * *

One of our nan's favourite programmes was the American western series *Bonanza*. One Sunday, an hour before it was due to start, she stood up and said she felt a little tired.

'I'm going to have a little sleep, Christine,' she said. 'Wake me up when *Bonanza* starts.'

She ruffled my hair as she walked past me and went into the bedroom. But an hour later, when Granddad went to wake her up, he couldn't. In a panic, he called for me to fetch Mrs Dennis, our next door neighbour. Mrs Dennis couldn't wake Nan either, so told me to fetch my mum. I remember sulking as I was now convinced I was going to miss *Bonanza*.

Within a few minutes, an ambulance came and the two medics managed to wake Nan up. She looked bewildered and said all she wanted to do was go to sleep. Within 10 minutes, the ambulance men had Nan on a stretcher and were taking her off to hospital.

The ambulance men asked who was going with her and my mum reached for my hand. 'We'll go, Christine, we'll look after her, won't we?'

I nodded, only too pleased to be getting a ride in an ambulance.

I was so excited, I'd never been in an ambulance before. I was more interested in looking out of the black windows than noticing what was going on with Nan. I felt so important at the hospital when the doors to the ambulance opened and people were rushing around everywhere. We were met by a doctor who walked alongside Nan's trolley right the way to the ward through miles and miles of corridors. By now, Nan had fallen asleep again.

The doctor drew the curtains round her bed and I was sent outside. He examined her for what seemed like hours, but eventually a nurse came to get me and I was let back in to see Nan. The ward was now in darkness except for Nan's bed that had curtains around it. It was the only part of the ward with a light and the curtains seemed almost radioactive as they shimmered in the darkness of the room. The nurse pulled back the curtain and Nan was sitting up in bed with a cup of tea. She asked me if I wanted some tea. I shook my head, just relieved that Nan was OK.

I remember Mum's worried face. We were only allowed to say goodnight then we had to go. I reached up to give Nan a kiss. Nan stroked my head and told me to be a good girl and she would see us all tomorrow. Just before we left, she said, 'Christine, I haven't got me glasses, so when you get home put them in your coat pocket and you can bring them in tomorrow.'

Nan gave us both a kiss goodnight, smiled, then waved as we walked out of the ward. I remember wondering what all the fuss had been about. She's just a little tired, I thought to myself on the way home, wondering why they'd brought her into hospital just for that. I turned back to wave at Nan and walked out of the ward.

I never saw my lovely nan again.

The following day, I put my nan's glasses in my pocket as I prepared for a visit to the hospital. What I didn't know was that my nan had died in the early hours of the morning. Children then were told nothing about death. Before I knew it, we were all packed up ready to be sent off to Kirkby to an auntie we never really knew. Although Kirkby was just on the outskirts of Liverpool, to us it was like being sent to the other side of the world. I knew something was terribly wrong as I looked into the eyes of my mum and Granddad. Mrs Dennis and a few other neighbours had called in but no one told me anything. I kept asking when I could see Nan but they all ignored me or made me cups of sweet tea that I wouldn't drink.

Kirkby was different. There were no derelict houses for me and Brian to play in, just lots of fields. It was like being on holiday, except that I sensed something was wrong with Nan and couldn't settle. We came back home, to find that Granddad had disappeared. He'd gone to stay with our uncle Joey, my mum's brother. Mum cried day and night. If she wasn't crying, she would sit and just stare at the walls. I asked her a hundred times where Nan had gone, but she never answered, never even looked me in the eye.

For days I would go out looking for her, convinced she had simply got lost or had gone away because she had found out about Granddad. So Granddad had been right. I had made Nan die and that was why Mum never looked at me because it was me that had made Nan go away.

I had a key to Nan and Granddad's house and would let myself in and play 'Welcome To My World', our favourite song by Jim Reeves, and cry and pray and beg for her to come back home but she never did. I'd walk from room to room expecting to find her standing there, washing dishes or cleaning as if it had been a big horrible dream, but now everything was back to normal.

My nan's death left a huge void in my life. I couldn't cope with not seeing her every day, not sleeping with her every night, not touching her and cuddling her, not hearing her voice or smelling her beautiful nan smell. But, most of all, I couldn't cope because of the guilt.

I was convinced I'd sent her away.

This abyss of emptiness without my nan was crushing me. And, although you might find this hard to believe, I was missing Granddad too.

I still believed I'd driven Nan away, so I continued to scour the length and breadth of Liverpool 8 looking for her. One day, still clutching her glasses in my hand, I was walking across waste ground at the back of Crown Street. A kindly old lady asked me what I was doing. When I told her I was looking for my nan, she asked me if I wanted to come to the Windsor Hall Sunday school and see if I could find Jesus.

'I can't,' I said. 'I have to find me nan, not Jesus.'

She smiled and asked me in again. She said I could look for Jesus while I was looking for my nan. I wasn't sure if I wanted to. If I couldn't find Nan, what chance did I have of finding Jesus? She introduced herself as Aunt Edie and told me I would get some orange juice and a chocolate biscuit inside. It was freezing cold and the temptation of the bribe was too strong, so I agreed and in I went.

The following Sunday, I took Brian and over the coming weeks we were regular attenders. Aunt Edie explained that Jesus forgave everyone, so I thought maybe he would forgive me for being so wicked that it made my nan go away.

Every Sunday, Brian and me would sit and listen in awe about the stories of Jesus – how kind he was and how he loved everyone no matter who they were or what they'd done, or what colour they were, or what language they talked. His father, God, understood all languages and listened to everyone's prayers in the whole world. I started praying every night, begging him to take my nightmares away and to send Nan back home.

Some weeks we would be given beautiful pictures of Jesus and we would run all the way back home at the end of the Sunday school lesson to give our mum the pictures. She would fold them up and slip them between the pages of her Bible.

But still the absence of my nan lay heavy in my heart. So, one Sunday, I showed my nan's glasses to Aunt Edie and asked her if Nan was with Jesus. She smiled and said yes. I asked if our nan had her glasses with her would she be able to see the way home and come back. Aunt Edie said that my nan didn't need her glasses any more because she was in heaven. I told Aunt Edie that Nan couldn't see properly without her glasses so how did she get to heaven in the first place? And what if she got on the wrong bus because she couldn't see the number on the front without her glasses? She still wouldn't be able to see where she was going, even though the hospital had given her two new eyes.

Aunt Edie thought for a moment.

'Well, Christine, have you ever fallen asleep on the settee or the chair and when you woke up you were in bed?'

'Yes, lots of times, Aunt Edie.'

She smiled. 'Dying is like falling into an eternal sleep. Then, when you fall asleep, Jesus comes down to pick you up and carries you up to heaven. Then, when you wake up, you're there. So you don't need glasses or a map or a bus.'

I thought I understood… but I still felt a bit confused. Aunt Edie clearly didn't know our nan because our nan wouldn't just go off with Jesus like that. So I started thinking I wanted to go to heaven. I could take Nan her glasses, then I could see Jesus, and so could Nan, and then we could both come back home.

But first I needed to die, and how do you do that?

I prayed to Jesus and God that I wanted to die and go to heaven to see Nan. I would lie on the chair and try to force myself to go to sleep, squeezing my eyes tight shut pretending to be asleep and waiting for Jesus to come and pick me up. Occasionally, I'd sneak a peek from one eye to see if he was coming.

But Jesus never came and I still wasn't in heaven. Night after night, I lay in bed and prayed I would die but it never worked. At this rate, I'd never see me nan.

I was in the pictures one Saturday watching the cowboy film with Brian and counting up how many people were killed. They would all be going to heaven. I was jealous. I didn't have a gun so I couldn't get shot but I watched the sheriff hang some of the baddies. That's it, I thought, I'll hang myself; that'll be easy. I didn't have the posh rope like the sheriff had but my mum had loads of tights back home that would make a good rope.

I went home straight away and sneaked into my mum's room. After searching in her wardrobe where she kept the clothes, at last I felt tights in my hands and pulled them out.

'Not long now, Nan, see you soon.'

I passed Mum in the living room; she was fast asleep on the chair and I sneaked into the back kitchen. I put Nan's glasses in my pocket. Now my plan was nearly complete, as I wrapped one leg of the nylon tights around my neck and tied them in a tight knot.

The kitchen window was small with a large steel clasp that jutted out. It was a perfect size to tie the other foot of the tights around and more than strong enough to take my weight. I climbed up on the window ledge and tied a double knot around the clasp and tugged hard to make sure it was securely fastened.

Then I jumped off. There was a huge crash as I cannoned into the door of the kitchen sink but the legs of the tights and the window frame held firm.

Fuck, did it hurt.

I thought my head was being ripped from my shoulders. My whole face felt like it would burst, and that my eyes could pop out of my head. I kicked involuntarily to try to get a foothold on the kitchen floor. I'd judged the length of the tights well and realised I was about a foot short of the floor. The more I struggled, the more I couldn't breathe, but, for a moment, I was pleased at how things were going, as this sort of pain and discomfort surely meant I would die and I would be off to heaven soon where I would see my lovely nan. But the pain was so great I began to change my mind. I didn't want to go to heaven after all.

My mum burst through the kitchen door screaming. She reached for a kitchen knife and started hacking and sawing through the tights. I fell into a heap on the kitchen floor coughing and spluttering but cursing my mother as she ripped the tights from my neck. She'd stopped me going to meet Nan in heaven.

'What are you doing, you fucking dopey bastard?' she screamed, as she lashed out at me.

I didn't know what was hurting more, my neck or the blows from my mother. My throat was that sore I couldn't answer her. I tried to explain my plan but I couldn't even speak – as I tried to swallow to moisten my throat it felt like I was swallowing glass.

Mum thought I must have lost the plot big time. After a few days, I had to go and see a special doctor. Mum took me into the surgery but stayed outside while he spoke to me. He asked me why I wanted to kill myself, but I didn't even know what killing myself meant. Kill myself, was he stupid? I just wanted to go and give my nan her glasses so she could come home.

That didn't seem to be the answer the doctor wanted. He showed me patterns of blobs of ink on pieces of card.

'What do you see in this picture, Christine?'

I looked at the blob of ink. It looked like a blob of ink. He put it to one side and showed me another shape.

'What do you see here?'

'A blob of ink.'

And another shape.

I studied it hard. 'A blob of ink.'

And another.

'Do you think your pen's leaking?'

He ignored me, and showed me another.

'A blob of ink.'

All wrong answers. By now, the doctor had made his diagnosis, and decided exactly what it was that a suicidal young girl with no imagination needed in order to move on with her life. I remember him scribbling furiously as I left the room.

CHAPTER SEVEN

FAR FROM HOME

I looked to heaven and tried to pray;
But or ever a prayer had gusht,
A wicked whisper came, and made
My heart as dry as dust.

After my failed suicide attempt that wasn't really a suicide attempt, I needed my family and, above all, familiar surroundings. I began to realise that I had done something stupid and really serious but all I had wanted to do was to go and see my nan. The doctor's questions had frightened me, and I was still in fear of my granddad, even though he still hadn't returned from Uncle Joey's. At least the doctor would make me better. One Saturday morning, Mum received his reply, and, as she opened the envelope, I waited to hear about his miracle cure.

His suggestion was a month in a convalescent home in Wales, run by nuns. He was sending me away from Mum and Dad and my brothers, my neighbours and friends. The doctor was punishing me, sending me to prison.

I was mortified and begged my mum not to send me. I had never been away from home before, except to Kirkby for a few days when Nan had died. I could tell Mum didn't want me to go either but the advice of the doctor in those days was like the word of God. If the doctor had said, 'Throw her off the nearest bridge,' then that's what she would have done.

Mum tried to convince me the doctor was right. She explained that they would help me to eat again. Two weeks since my failed attempt to see Nan, all I could eat was soup. Even eating a banana was like trying to swallow a football. To this day I can't swallow anything with a skin on like an apple and even if I have fish and chips I pull the batter off first.

One Saturday morning, Mum put me on the bus to Wales. I was in tears and begged her not to make me go, right up to the point where the bus doors closed. She ignored me and gave the instructions to the driver that I had to get off in Prestatyn at a place called Ffrith Beach. I sat at the back of the bus shaking my head, clawing desperately at the window as Mum waved me off with the tears welling up in her eyes. I sobbed all the way to Wales.

I was met at the other end by Sister Geraldine, a lady about the same age as my mum. She was dressed in a grey skirt, grey cardigan and white blouse with a gold crucifix and the customary grey wimple. She seemed nice enough and even held my hand as we walked about a mile to the convalescent home. I had imagined the building would look like a hospital but it didn't; it was more like a huge mansion set in beautiful gardens with views of the beach down below. Perhaps it wouldn't be so bad after all, I thought, as I walked through the door.

Mum had told me about the nuns, how kind they were, and how close they were to God and Jesus. So maybe they could help me find Nan.

Sister Geraldine took me in to see the Mother Superior, an elderly nun dressed identically to the sister, except her gold crucifix was bigger. The Mother Superior proceeded to interview me, not unlike the doctor had done; at one point, I expected her to get the blobs of ink out. She asked me over and over again about trying to kill myself and I told her all about my nan and that I hadn't wanted to die. She said I had sinned trying to take my life and ended up shouting at me. She asked me if I had any problems and all I could think of was that I couldn't eat properly. She wrote that down on a notepad and picked up the telephone to summon Sister Geraldine who showed me to my bedroom. I shared my room with three other girls who hardly spoke. It was as if everyone had taken a vow of silence. That suited me as it was still an effort to speak more than a few words.

I lay awake most of the night praying to Jesus to tell my nan that I was sorry for making her go away and asking if he could possibly send me back home. Despite the problems there, I was missing it so much.

Homesick, I told the Mother Superior the next morning that I wanted to go home. That didn't go down too well. She called me ungrateful and said I was there to get better and to give my parents a break. I had been selfish when I tried to kill myself, and I was being selfish now. She shouted at me to get out and start to think about others for a change. I left in tears with my tail well and truly between my legs.

Mealtimes were the worst because we were instructed to finish whatever was on our plates whether we liked the food or not. We were told that all food was a gift from God and to leave even the tiniest scrap on our plates was an insult to him. That was fine, but clearly no one had told the other nuns about my throat, and that I'd been on liquids for two weeks. So they gave me exactly the same food as the other girls.

The first meal was sausage and mashed potatoes. The mash was fine but eating the sausages was an impossibility. I cut the skin from one sausage and tried to swallow a tiny, tiny piece of the meat. It was like swallowing a hot poker and when it got to the back of my throat it seemed to close up in a spasm. I immediately gagged and spat it out. Sister Geraldine came over and I explained to her that I couldn't swallow. She asked me if I'd told Mother Superior, and I said I had. So Sister Geraldine walked over to where Mother Superior sat eating her dinner with some of the other nuns. When she came back, she said that Mother Superior said I had to try eating properly sooner or later and that I still had to clear my plate.

I managed to clear my plate by offloading the sausages to two other girls. That was a big mistake because when Mother Superior saw my empty plate she believed I had been able to eat everything. She looked at me and smiled, then looked at the ceiling and said, 'Praise the Lord.'

Anything I couldn't eat or couldn't offload to the other girls, I simply threw on the floor, making sure I chucked it as far as possible so as not to arouse any suspicion. Any meat, roast potatoes, chips, peas, carrots and cabbage would end up under the communal dining table seating about 30 girls. It worked fine and after a few days I didn't even bother to try to give the food away.

After about five days, I was given a huge bowl of the foulest pudding I had ever tasted. It was called tapioca, but it looked and felt like frogspawn, and, although it slipped down my throat quite nicely, I retched and nearly choked. It was simply awful and I started to cough, alerting Mother Superior who quickly walked over.

'What's the problem, Christine?'

'That, Sister.' I pointed to the bowl. 'It's horrible.'

Mother Superior leaned over me. 'How dare you,' she whispered. 'The good Lord does not provide anything horrible.'

'But, Sister, it's...'

'Eat it up now.'

She handed me the spoon and stood over me. I put it back on the table, closed my mouth and shook my head. She scooped up a spoonful of tapioca and tried to force the spoon into my mouth. I simply kept turning my head as the spoon came my way. Mother Superior was now turning bright red with anger and she grabbed a handful of my hair.

'Don't you know there are little boys and girls in Africa starving?'

'Give it to them then,' I said.

Mother Superior snapped and thrust the spoon towards me while forcing my mouth open with a finger and thumb pressing into each cheek. I could feel the spoon between my teeth, but she forced it in even deeper and it rasped against the back of my throat. The agony was almost unbearable, and as she tipped the spoon the tapioca slid down into my throat and settled on my stomach.

Mother Superior thought she'd won. But then she didn't know what hit her. It was projectile vomit. Her wimple, her crisp white blouse and her grey cardigan were covered in the stuff: tapioca mixed with mashed potato, gravy and some well-chewed cauliflower had flown involuntarily out of my mouth with the force of Niagara Falls. It really was an accident. I didn't mean to bring all that up, though I must confess I was responsible for where I directed it.

As Mother Superior stood there, covered in vomit and still holding the spoon, I thought about apologising but figured it would be a waste of time. I'd have been lying had I said sorry. The old bitch deserved it.

She staggered out of the dining hall, followed by two of the nuns, while another two set about cleaning the stinking pool of vomit still in the middle of the floor. Ten minutes later, she returned all cleaned up.

She walked over to where I sat and lifted me from my seat by the scruff of my neck. She forced me to the middle of the room, lifted up my skirt, exposing my bare legs and proceeded to beat me with her hard leathery hands. She slapped me mercilessly as I begged her to stop but it went on and on. I felt like I was back in my granddad's house, with him playing the choking game with Brian. My legs were on fire, numb and yet throbbing at the same time, and still she wouldn't stop. I called out to Sister Geraldine for help, but she just looked the other way. I tried God and Jesus again but, as always, they ignored me.

Mother Superior slapped me until the sheer pain and desperation caused me to wet myself. She hadn't realised this, and continued to slap me. She ended up slipping in the pool of urine just as she became aware that she was beating me with a warm, wet hand. She sat exhausted in a pool of wet piss as two nuns lifted her from the floor and took her away to be cleaned up for the second time that day.

But my punishment wasn't over. Mother Superior cleared the dining hall and made me clean 'my mess' up. She stripped me out of my dirty clothing and made me bend over on my hands and knees while she stood over me, as I wiped up the cold urine with a cloth and squeezed it into a bucket. Afterwards, she threw me into a freezing cold shower and sent me to my room. I shivered and cried myself to sleep, praying that my ordeal at the hands of the sisters of God would soon be over.

The next morning, I could hardly lift myself from my bed. My legs felt as if they'd been trampled on by a hundred horses. My room-mates helped me into a hot bath and I lay there for about 30 minutes which seemed to ease the pain a little.

Mother Superior watched me like a hawk for the rest of my stay. Several days later, she caught me throwing food on the floor and beat me again, until Sister Geraldine intervened and told her to look carefully at my legs that she was battering. They were black and blue and swollen to twice their normal size. I wonder if Mother Superior even realised she had gone too far. I never threw food on the floor again; I was so terrified of further punishment. Instead, I simply sneaked the food I couldn't eat into my pockets and flushed it down the toilets. Mother Superior made a point of checking my plate after each meal, convinced she had won the war. She hadn't.

When Mum met me off the bus from Wales some weeks later, I threw myself into her arms and sobbed like a baby, pleading with her never to send me to that place again. Religion, don't make me laugh. Some of those nuns gave religion a bad name, and one in particular was one of the most evil bastards I have ever come across.

It was only after my awful experiences at the convalescent home that I really understood that Nan was gone forever. I stopped looking for her. I never wanted to go back to that place in Wales ever again, so another attempt at dying was out of the question. So I suppose some good came out of that awful experience. But what was that psychiatrist thinking of, sending a small girl who'd never even been away on holiday to a place like that?

Granddad was still away at Uncle Joey's and I'd heard Mum and Dad talking about him on more than one occasion. They said he wasn't right and couldn't accept Nan's death. When he returned home, he was a different man. A piece of him had died with Nan. He came to live with us at 3C and I was scared in case I had to share a bed with him. I needn't have worried. Granddad got a room of his own, and me and my brothers all shared the same bed in a different one.

He would never return to his former home and from that day until the day he died, over Christmas 1974, he would never again lay a hand on me or Brian. I'd like to say we had our normal granddad back but we didn't; he'd changed, he had a heavy heart. Perhaps he believed it was his actions that had taken Nan away, but I didn't know, and I never got the chance to ask him.

I wish I could have sat down with him with some tea and cake, and said to him, 'You know what? I had this strangest dream that you did these things to me and I can't understand why. I looked up to you as something special, something really special, and sometimes I feel sick. I loved you, Granddad, but I didn't want to love you the way you loved me back.'

I do forgive him, I do. And if I could just sit for a second or a minute or an hour with him, I'd hold his hand between my hands and say it's OK now, it doesn't matter any more. You are my granddad and I love you. I love you. And I don't understand what happened, or why it happened, and now I don't think I want to understand. But it's OK now, it's over and I forgive you.

Above left: Little Christine Murray, just five months old.

Above right: This photo's terrible but I wanted to include it as it shows me in my first stage role as one of Ken Dodd's diddymen. That's me, second from the left in the flat cap, grinning like a Cheshire cat. Lovely Doddy even signed my photo on the back for me.

Below: With my brothers: Ian's on the left and I'm holding David on my knee. Brian, my hero, is on the right.

Above left: Mum and Dad with our Jason in sunny Blackpool.

Above right: With my gorgeous mum and wonderful brother, Ian.

Below: With my lovely Aunty Jean, who was a great support to me when I was travelling the country doing my stand-up gigs.

Snaps from the Murray family album.

Above left: That's me, top middle, with Ian on the left and David on the right. Mum and Dad are in the middle; my Hayley is sat on my mum's knee and that's my elder daughter Tracy next to my little brother Jason.

Above right: Little Hayley with my nan, Lizzie.

Below: My little brother Jason, my daughter Tracy with her little sister Hayley on her knee and my brother David in the checked shirt. Funny how this looks so like the photo on the first page where I'm holding David on my knee.

I was gobsmacked when I landed the role of Maggie Conlan in Ken Loach's *Ladybird, Ladybird*. Ken Loach and Sally Hibbin celebrated my birthday while we were filming and, *below right*, me and Sally in Dublin to promote the film.

Ladybird, Ladybird exorcised all the demons I had inside me.

Above and below left: Scenes from the film, in which Vladimir Vega played Jorge.

Below right: Winning the award for Best Foreign Actress in Barcelona. I thought this giant statue was the award and wondered how I was going to get that on the plane and through customs!

Above: Having a ball in *Brazen Hussies* with Julie Walters.   *Above left © Rex Features*

Below left: With my best friend in the whole world, Margie Jones, and my daughter, Hayley.

Below right: With Billie Whitelaw.

Above left: Filming *Dockers*, Jimmy McGovern's hard-hitting TV drama.

Above right: With the hugely talented Mr McGovern.

Below: At the BAFTAs with Joanna Lumley and the woman on whom my character in *Dockers* was based.

Above left: With John McArdle in *Peak Practice*.

Above right: My finest hour! Playing a dead body in *Dalziel and Pascoe*.

Below: At the wrap party for *The Butterfly Collectors* with the wonderful – and now, tragically, late – Pete Postlethwaite.

Is that wrong? I don't know.

So many things, so many memories to try to filter in and out of your life.

CHAPTER EIGHT

EDUCATING CRISSY

*And now this spell was snapped: once more
I viewed the ocean green,
And looked far forth, yet little saw
Of what had else been seen – ...*

It was 1969. Man had landed on the moon. Neil Armstrong's words – 'The eagle has landed' – are unforgettable to anyone over 45 who watched those grainy black and white TV pictures of Apollo 11 landing there. Poor Dad didn't see much of it though; he was trying to get a good picture by hanging over the window ledge and balancing the aerial out of the window with a metal coat hanger. He kept shouting down, 'Is that it, is that it?' We'd be nodding our heads, so he'd try and hold the aerial in exactly the same place, but we weren't nodding that the picture was OK. We were nodding because the vertical hold on the telly was knackered and our heads were going up and down just to keep in time with the motion of the picture.

At this time, Mum was still bad with her nerves, really bad, and I remember Dad spending a lot of time home from work. After Dad's accident, when he was hit with a car while delivering parcels, he couldn't return to that job, so went to work at Armey and Layfields, coincidentally the same factory where the men had thrown those orange boxes down from the roof. Armey and Layfields produced confectionery of sorts and Dad worked preparing marzipan for a big machine; he used to stink of the stuff sometimes. It was obviously not that well paid as we still seemed to struggle.

* * *

It was around 1969 that I took my first tentative steps on the stage. Dad was looking through the *Liverpool Echo*, ignoring Granddad's moans that he was taking too long with it.

Dad said that Ken Dodd was holding auditions at the Royal Court in Liverpool for Diddy Men. Ken Dodd was famous; he was on telly every Sunday with his Diddy Men: children dressed up to look like little dwarfs who would sing and dance and clown around. We watched them every week.

'Why don't you go, our Christine?' Dad said.

Me? I couldn't dance or even sing; what was the point? But as I lay awake in bed that night I dreamed of superstardom. Anyway, even if I didn't make it, at least I might meet Ken Dodd, and I'd never met anyone famous before. I also thought it might get me away for a night or two, out of the house, and away from Granddad.

My chance came the following Saturday. Mum had told me I would need to sing a song at the audition and dance a little. So I'd practised performing Millie Small's 'My Boy Lollipop'.

Mum gave me a bottle of water and the money for my bus fare into Liverpool. I told the bus driver where I had to get off and thankfully he remembered to tell me as I just sat looking out of the window in a daze.

The queue down at the Royal Court stretched right around

the theatre. There were hundreds of hopeful kids standing with their mums and dads, but I was on my own, so I pushed in to the queue and managed to get quite near the front. It was just as well because, five minutes before the doors opened, a man came and told about 200 children behind me that they wouldn't be getting in. They looked so disappointed – some were even in tears.

Once inside the theatre I kind of tagged on to a group of about 12 kids. They were all dressed up, looked quite professional and didn't seem to notice me hanging around.

Our group was called forward by a lady who had white hair and we were ushered towards the back of the stage.

At the front of the stage, a woman sat at a table with a book taking names. I pushed myself to the front of the stage and stood on my own. Without even looking up, the lady said, 'Name?'

'Christine Murray.'

'Age?'

'Eleven.'

I was just about to burst with excitement when she asked, 'Name of your dance school please?'

Dance school, I thought, what dance school?

She looked up and peered over the top of her glasses as they slid down the bridge of her nose. 'You are with a dancing school?' she said.

Dad never said anything about a bloody dancing school. All I saw was the picture of Ken Dodd and his Diddy Men in the *Echo*, with a big section of words underneath. I wished with all my heart that I had been able to read the article. But of course I couldn't read it; it was just a series of jumbled-up letters that made no sense at all. If I could have read those words, perhaps I would have known that you needed to be a member of a dance school, otherwise there was no point in turning up. I had wasted my time and my bus money coming into Liverpool. I froze, and wondered if I could make something up. I couldn't think. Then a voice from behind me said, 'What have I told you about wandering off?'

The lady who had spoken walked over to me and placed a hand on my shoulder. She looked at the lady with the glasses and announced, 'Vera Corrine Dancing School.' She smiled, then winked at me and walked off to the side of the stage.

'What are you going to sing, Christine?' the lady with the glasses asked.

'"My Boy Lollipop" by Millie Small,' I replied.

Accompanied by a piano at the side of the stage, I began to sing. I loved every second of my routine and, while the first half-minute of my performance was rather laboured and nervy, by the end of the song I was performing like a professional on Broadway. At least I thought so anyway. And Vera Corrine seemed to agree, because, at the end, she put her arm round me as she took me to one side.

'So, miss,' she said, 'you fancy yourself as a dancer then?'

I shrugged my shoulders. 'I don't know, but I like Pan's People on *Top of the Pops*.'

Vera Corrine burst out laughing. 'I watched you, wriggling and squirming your way through to the front of the stage, and I saw that look in your eye.'

'What look?'

'*That* look: eagerness, excitement, and I saw how much you enjoyed your five minutes of fame out there.'

She pointed to the lady with the glasses. 'She saw the look too.'

'She did?'

'And she enjoyed your performance.'

'She did?'

By now, I was beginning to enjoy myself. This lady was making me feel good. In a roundabout way, she was telling me that I was good at something. The feeling was alien to me – in all the years I'd been at school, not one teacher had ever told me I'd been good at anything.

'So what's your name, did you say?'

'It's Christine, miss.'

'Well, Christine, mine is Vera, but the girls call me Auntie Vera.'

And then she said the nicest words I had ever heard:

'Christine, would you like to join my dancing school?'

I was speechless, so dumbfounded I couldn't answer her, but the following Saturday I did indeed join her dancing school in the Dingle district of Liverpool. There were lots of girls there tap-dancing in the corner, and I was absolutely mesmerised as I watched them practising their moves. Then we were told that three of the Vera Corrine Dancing School had made the grade after the Royal Court auditions, and been chosen to be Ken Dodd's Diddy Men.

The excitement and anticipation was electric. The mothers fussing over the tap-dancers could hardly wait until the end of the practice session when the 'Diddy Men' would be announced. There were at least 45 hopeful girls, so the odds were not good, but, when the name Christine Murray was read out as the final Diddy Man, I could have floated up to the ceiling. Auntie Vera went on to say everyone had performed well and there had to be losers as well as winners.

So I'd made it into showbiz. I was one of Ken Dodd's Diddy Men.

I was at Vera Corrine's School of Dancing for about two years and loved every minute of it. I wasn't exactly Ginger Rogers but I was OK. Auntie Vera was a teacher but not like the teachers I'd experienced at school; she was genuinely interested in what she was doing and loved every one of her pupils like a daughter. She'd be at every single show we performed, and she never missed a Diddy Men performance that we'd give at parks and theatres in and around Liverpool. I wasn't ever chosen to appear on television with Ken Dodd – that honour went to a select few – but it didn't matter. I was still a Diddy Man and, believe me, in Liverpool that was rather special.

***

When I was nearly 12 years old, I went to Paddington Comprehensive. It was like a whole new world and I was a little apprehensive and nervous about going as I'd heard rumours about the initiation ceremonies performed on newcomers. The school had a uniform and I heard Mum and Dad saying we qualified for a grant to buy it. When Dad brought my uniform home, trying it on was so exciting. I paraded in front of Mum and Dad, showing off doing twirls and curtsies.

My new school was huge, but it felt like the system and the teachers had simply given up on us. I couldn't read as the teachers at my primary class had failed me, so I was put into what was called the progress class, which it turned out was for the no-hopers, the dunces, the boys and girls who were as thick as a brick. Progress class? Surely they could have found a better name than that!

Some of the teachers did try to help, but the majority either just pretended to teach us or gave up before they'd even started.

I recall a chemistry teacher who kept the door to his labs locked so that we had to queue up before each lesson. He'd turn up about 20 minutes late always with the greeting: 'Line up, you horrible little specimens.'

He marched us in military fashion and made us sit down at the huge lab desks. He'd then roar in an intimidating voice, 'Don't touch anything, don't touch the gas taps or the water taps or even the benches.' We'd then get a five-minute lecture on how useless we were and how we didn't deserve to be at school and he'd waffle on about how good and appreciative his other classes were, and towards the end of the lesson he'd give a very half-hearted attempt at a lecture on oxygen or gas or the make-up of a chemical.

During one of these lectures, one girl, Susan Haygan, wondered what it would be like to shove the Bunsen burner gas tube up her nose and turn it on. For two or three minutes, I watched fascinated as she floated to a different galaxy. She had a satisfied smile on her face just before she crashed unconscious to the floor with the tube still sticking out of her left nostril. The teacher went apeshit, unable to decide whether to batter her or resuscitate her. He finally brought her round by throwing a cup of ice cold water in her face. When the bell went for the end of the lesson, he gave an audible sigh of relief, but still couldn't resist screaming, 'Don't touch anything,' as we shuffled off to our next lesson.

One day in progress class, we spent a whole lesson copying out the weekly lesson timetable from the blackboard. That was fine, I could copy anything and any words, no problem whatsoever. The only thing I couldn't do was read those words once I had copied them. So I'd wander round the corridors wondering what the letters 'm.a.t.h.e.m.a.t.i.c.s' meant until a teacher would find me and point me in the right direction. Some lessons I would miss altogether and some days I would just take off home. Mum never seemed to mind; I'd tell her my lessons were finished for the day and she'd be grateful for the helping hands looking after my little brothers.

School in general seemed to me to be about humiliation and discrimination of the poor kids. I think things are a little better nowadays, but back then everyone knew the families and the kids who had nothing. Even at lunchtime there were three sittings; the children on free dinners were last and many days there would be nothing left. The other children with full bellies would taunt and tease us with names and comments and rub their stomachs and lick their lips. One day I asked a dinner lady why there was nothing left. She said, 'Tell your dad to get out of his lazy bed and get a job and he'd be able to pay for it.' I tried to explain that my dad already had a job but she just pushed me along the queue to the next dinner lady, where I managed to salvage a few chips and a piece of bread and butter for my dinner.

When the time came for school photographs, we'd all line up and the teacher would go along the kids picking two or three out and removing them from the line-up. I was always one of them and asked one day why I was always chosen and why I could never get my picture taken. In front of the whole class, the twat announced it was because my dad couldn't afford to buy the school photographs anyway so what was the point of including me. We never had a camera at home either so I haven't even got one picture of myself in that uniform that I was so proud to pull on those first few weeks.

My pride quickly evaporated as the humiliation continued. One day in class, the teacher asked me if my mum knew that electricity had been invented.

I replied, 'Of course she does, sir.'

'Ask her why she hasn't ironed your uniform then,' he said, grinning, as the rest of my classmates started laughing.

There was a simple explanation: our old iron was broken and we just couldn't afford another one, especially as Dad was spending even more time at home looking after Mum, sometimes losing two or three days' pay every week.

I leaped to her defence. 'How dare you say that about me mum.'

I'd dared to answer him back, and the wooden blackboard rubber sailed through the air and hit me on the shoulder as it exploded into a cloud of dust. I stood up and threw it back. 'Fuck off, you dickhead.'

I kept him at bay for at least five minutes as we ran between the desks but eventually he caught up with me. He marched me to the head's office and I was expelled for a week. It suited me just fine.

That week, I looked after Granddad, who by now was quite ill, but it was the same week that we learned that our tenements were being knocked down and we would have to move. I was shell-shocked; all I had ever known was life in the tenements. Within a few weeks, we had the order to move, and Dad told us with a smile that our new house was to be on two floors. Wow.

Our new home was at Baslow Walk. It was part of a new development, a housing estate built on Chatsworth Street. I remember Mum being excited and telling us she had longed to get out of our tenements. I couldn't help shedding a few tears of sadness, though, as I walked alongside the pram full of our clothes with Mum and my brothers. I had many happy memories of Windsor Gardens but I also felt I was leaving the nightmares behind. By now, Granddad hardly had the strength to walk. My dad and Uncle Pip moved the bigger things like the beds and sofas on the back of a coal wagon covered in an old blanket to keep our few sticks of furniture clean. They walked just in front of us.

Our new house at Baslow Walk was massive, a real change from living at Windsor Gardens. In the kitchen there was a stainless-steel sink unit and a fully fitted kitchen, a big change from Windsor Gardens where we only had a larder cupboard and two shelves, which were knackered!

Now we'd have four bedrooms, a bathroom upstairs and a toilet downstairs. I remember thinking we were really posh. I'd never be taunted as a 'poor kid' at school ever again. Perhaps we could even pay for school dinners and I'd be first in the queue. Maybe we'd get a new iron…

The move seemed to give Mum a new lease of life; she was so happy and so were we. There was lots of room now, even though it looked quite bare because we didn't have much furniture. It didn't matter.

A few hours after we moved in, Dad returned with Granddad who by this time was confined to a wheelchair. Granddad came into the huge living room moaning and muttering that Dad had pushed him too fast or too slow and that he didn't want him living there anyway.

'Shut up, ya moanin' auld get,' Dad would shout before walking into another room. Dad was so easy-going and placid and did anything that Mum said, but it seemed he could do no right with Granddad. Granddad moaned constantly. His bed had been made up in the corner of the big lounge as getting him up flights of stairs was a big effort. I noticed Mum was placing some sheets and blankets and a pillow on the settee next to Granddad's bed.

'Who's sleeping there?' I asked.

She turned to me and frowned. 'You'll have to look after him, our Christine,' she said. 'You're quite capable and old enough. He might need things through the night.'

I remember being disappointed that I wasn't getting a new bedroom.

CHAPTER NINE

THE END OF THE ANCIENT MARINER

He went like one that hath been stunned,
And is of sense forlorn;
A sadder and a wiser man
He rose the morrow morn.

Mum was crying and Dad was trying to comfort her. I more or less passed the doctor as he was leaving as I got home from school.

'Your granddad's had a stroke, Christine,' Dad said to me and I shrugged my shoulders. I didn't know what a stroke was. Granddad's bed was in the corner of our living room downstairs and I walked through and asked him how he was feeling. He didn't answer. I noticed a steel container on a frame beside his bed and a mask with tubes leading to a valve. Granddad was on oxygen. I'd never studied him so closely before, and he was little more than a bag of bones. Granddad was more or less paralysed by the stroke and even with a stick he could walk no more than a few feet. I cared for him during the night, and whenever he wanted something he used to prod me with the stick. He could no longer make it to the bathroom and they brought a commode in so he could go to the toilet.

The poor old bugger lost every shred of his dignity when he had to go on that thing. I can still see the anguish in his face as he faced up to the reality that he couldn't hold his shit in any longer. He'd bang his stick against the wall and grimace with a pained, twisted look on his face; it was like the House of Usher.

Day or night, I'd jump up and push the commode next to the bed. I'd help him on to it and we'd pull his pyjamas down to his knees. I'd leave the room as he completed the operation and give him his 10 minutes of privacy. The room was stinking every time I returned and Granddad would lean forward as I returned to wipe his bottom. He'd often apologise to me, saying he was sorry that he couldn't manage it himself. I'd struggle but lift him back into the bed and then empty the contents of the commode into the toilet. The first few times were the worst; after that, I think I just got used to it.

When Granddad went on oxygen, the doctor said that our ducted air central heating wasn't doing him any good and it would be advisable to have it removed and replaced with radiators. The very next morning, Dad was sent down to the council and instructed to tell them our old central heating had to go. The council agreed to take it all out but refused to pay for a replacement system; that was down to us. I remember Dad ranting in the kitchen a few weeks later as the workmen disconnected the pipes to the boiler that we didn't have the money for a new one.

He sipped at his cup of tea as he went on and on about the warmest house he'd ever set foot in and because of 'that auld get' he was back to living in an icebox again. Needless to say, we never found the extra money for the new system. Granddad tried to make amends by buying an electric bar fire out of his savings but still moaned on about our dad not doing anything for him and not liking him. Mum would always bring up the subject of the central heating whenever Granddad started moaning about Dad. She'd argue that, if Dad hadn't liked him, he wouldn't have allowed him to live there, and he certainly wouldn't have had the central heating taken out!

I hope that, despite his moaning, Granddad respected our dad, even though he never admitted it. But his health was worsening, and by now he was only going out once a week to collect his pension. I'd push him in his wheelchair up to the shops on Tunnel Road. The routine never changed. We'd collect his pension from the post office and stop off at the fishmonger's where he would buy two fresh crabs. He would make a point of choosing his own; the fish man would have five or six lined up and Granddad would check the size, the colour and the weight before eventually making his mind up. It was his last job, his last responsibility in life, and it was as if he was demonstrating to the world that he was still useful in some small way. After the fishmonger's, I'd push him down to the sweet shop where he'd buy half a pound of Uncle Joe's mint balls and that was it for another seven days. Back home he was lifted back into his bed at the back of the room. It was like he was one of the bed-bound grandparents in *Charlie and the Chocolate Factory*.

I had become his carer, in truth. I had to wash him, dress him and feed him with a spoon. What a turnaround. When I washed his hands, I'd cringe and feel sick. I knew where those hands had once been; I knew these were the very hands that had closed around poor Brian's throat and worse. His hands had turned into claws and I had to push my hand into his hand like a ball to open them up in order to wash them. The doctor had told us it was part of his physiotherapy and it had to be done at least twice every day. We never spoke as I manipulated his hands.

The silence between us was deafening... he knew exactly what I was thinking, he sensed my anxiety, but I just had to get on with it.

But I never wished him harm, despite what he had put me and my brother through. Not once did I look at the pathetic state that his life had become and think, 'Serves you right, you old bastard.' I had no bitterness; how could I? The ancient mariner was on his last legs; he was harmless, useless and sometimes I questioned whether the abuse had actually taken place. I wondered whether it had all been a big nasty dream as I sat and watched him barely able to speak.

Only once during those last few years did I ever get angry with him. I'll never forget it. It was Boxing Day 1974, and I was 16. In the night, he woke me with a poke of his stick, and I automatically went for his commode. As I pushed the commode towards him, he was shaking his head and beckoning me to come forward.

He wanted to speak to me. I looked at his hand and noticed that it was balled up worse than ever. It was 3.30 in the morning. I pushed the commode back to the bottom of his bed and leaned down to listen to what he had to say.

He really struggled to get the words out.

'I'm sorry,' he whispered gently. 'I'm sorry.'

He gasped for breath and I handed him his oxygen mask and switched it on. He took another few lungfuls of air before continuing.

'I'm sorry.'

The tears were welling up in his eyes by now. Was this the great confession, the apology for what he'd done to me and Brian?

'I'm sorry... I'm sorry... for not getting you anything for Christmas.'

'What?' I was incredulous.

'Sorry I haven't bought you anything for Christmas, Christine.'

I couldn't quite believe it. He had the nerve to apologise for not getting me a present after everything he'd done to me and my brother. I felt like choking him. He'd woken me up in the early hours of the morning to apologise about a fucking Christmas present he hadn't bought. I thought back to the weekly ritual of the choking game and the fear in Brian's eyes and those days where he caught me on my own and the sheer terror as he climbed on top of me.

For a few awful, awful seconds I hated him. Moments later, the feelings passed and he closed his eyes and drifted off to sleep.

A few days later, he woke me again. He was in a cold sweat, pointing at his oxygen cylinder, but in his eyes was a different kind of panic. He needed enormous strength just to whisper, 'I can't breathe.' The veins were bulging blue in his temple and he trembled all over, with sweat dripping from his chin. I placed his oxygen mask over his mouth and told him to calm down. He took several gulps of oxygen before relaxing a little. He turned to me as his eyes glazed over, removed the mask and whispered, 'I'm sorry.'

He closed his eyes and took some more deep breaths before repeating the exercise.

'I'm sorry,' he wheezed with his eyes firmly shut.

I didn't know what he was apologising for. Was it that bloody Christmas present again or was it something else?

'What is it, Granddad, why are you sorry?'

He turned to face me. He repeated his apology before closing his eyes.

'Sorry... sorry, Christine.'

He started to snore gently and I tried to wake him. I didn't want him to sleep, not this time; he had to tell me what he was sorry for.

'Granddad… Granddad.'

Something was wrong. Instinct told me to fetch Mum and we managed to wake Granddad up again, but as soon as he opened his eyes he began to panic, pointing at his oxygen mask and grasping at his throat. He was obviously in pain. Mum made me run outside to the payphone in the street to call Dr Densfang, the Malaysian doctor. Within 20 minutes, he was with us. He diagnosed a chest infection and gave Granddad something to calm him down. Dad came through with a cup of tea for everyone and we sat with Granddad while he fell back to sleep. Mum, Dad and me sat for an hour talking about Granddad and his illnesses. Mum sobbed most of the time while Dad caressed her shoulder. Dad may not have been a big man in terms of stature, but he had a huge heart and not a bad bone in his body. How many men could have gone through what he had gone through with Granddad and still sat with the ungrateful old bugger as he lay sleeping in the early hours of the morning without a bad word to say against him?

I had drifted off to sleep, but, when I awoke with a start, Mum and Dad were still there fussing over Granddad who was now awake and clearly distressed. I was sent down to the payphone for the second time that night and called Dr Densfang again. When I got back to the house, Mum made me go and sleep in her bed.

'Your dad and me will watch him,' she said. 'You get some sleep.'

It was a rare treat to sleep in a real bed instead of a settee and I jumped at the chance as I slipped up the stairs in the dark. By now I was knackered, the recent nights taking their toll. I looked into the room where my brothers were sleeping on the way to Mum's bed. They'd slept through everything and a gentle snore from Brian hummed around the room. I walked over, sat on the bed and gently stroked his brow.

It was daylight when Dad woke me and told me that Granddad had died.

The Ancient Mariner was no more.

CHAPTER TEN

ANOTHER ORDEAL

The Mariner, whose eye is bright,
Whose beard with age is hoar,
Is gone; and now the Wedding Guest
Turned from the bridegroom's door.

On hearing the news, I leaped out of bed and rushed downstairs. I could hear Mum crying her eyes out in the living room. As I ran through, she was draped over Granddad's body and Dad was doing all he could to comfort her.

Granddad was lying down on the bed, his face covered by a plain white cotton sheet.

'Let him breathe,' I said, and I pulled the sheet back. His face was grey, completely drained of life and I knew then he was dead. His eyes were closed and in the few hours since I had seen him it was as if they'd sunk another few inches deep into his skull. His cheekbones were prominent and I could make out the faint lines of every bone in his face. But worse, his mouth was wide open as if, right on the point of death, he'd wanted to cry out loud, wanted to say something.

I tried to close his mouth but Dad moved me away and covered his face once more with the sheet.

'No,' I cried out, 'let him breathe, let him breathe.'

I broke down sobbing as an overwhelming pain of pity filled my heart. At the same time, an anger pounded in my chest. He'd died so suddenly, with no explanation or apology for what he'd done, and all I could think of was that bloody Christmas present. How could he die without talking to Brian and me? How dare he? Why, Granddad, why?

I knelt down beside the bed, pulled the sheet back and took hold of his hand. It was a claw, more like an eagle's talons than a hand. I tried to open it like I had when I washed him, but each time I took my hand away it balled up into a claw again. I just wanted to hold my granddad's hand. Was that too much to ask?

I lay sobbing with Mum for at least an hour. This was the worst day of my life.

I couldn't accept that Granddad was dead. I kept taking the sheet away to see if it looked different, or if he was breathing. In the end, Dad took me away into the kitchen and plied me with cups of hot sweet tea. Throughout the day, I kept returning to Granddad's dead body lying on the bed but no longer wanted to look at his face. I reassured myself by imagining it was the monster who had died and all that was left was the body of my granddad who I had once loved.

At around dinner time, the friends and family, neighbours and well-wishers started turning up at the house. Word had leaked out on the grapevine. Dad welcomed them all with tea, and they sat down with my mum and tried to comfort her. People were coming into our house who I'd never ever seen before: neighbours that hadn't called in to see Granddad for months, even years. Some of them even wanted to see his dead body, but I refused to let anyone go near him.

'Get out,' I shouted, 'go away.'

Dad explained that I was mourning. Mum was oblivious and just sat and stared at the shape underneath the white cotton sheet, every few minutes bursting into tears. Later that day, Granddad's body was taken away to the funeral parlour.

Two days before the funeral, Mum sent me to one of the neighbours' houses for some tea. Dad was at work and Mum didn't have the energy or heart to leave the house. She was crying almost continuously. The door to the neighbour's house was open as it always was and I walked in as usual.

'Joan,' I shouted, 'Joan…' (I have changed the name of our neighbour for reasons that will become clear shortly.)

I was aware of the door closing behind me and I turned. A man who I'd never seen before had closed it and was placing a brass chain across the door. I immediately became concerned and on the defensive.

'Where's Joan?' I asked.

'She's not in,' he replied.

I wondered why he'd chained the door. Had he locked me in or had he done it to keep someone out?

'I'm Joan's son-in-law. Who are you?' He stepped forward and he offered his hand. I shook it politely.

'Christine Murray.'

'How old are you, Christine?'

'Sixteen.'

'You're very pretty, Christine.'

He walked towards me. He wasn't looking at my face; he was looking me up and down and had a look on his face that Granddad used to get.

'Ever been with a boy before?' he asked.

I didn't answer that, but said, 'I'm going home if Joan's not in. My mum will be wondering where I am.'

I walked towards the chained door, but he blocked my path.

I dodged him, but as I reached the door I felt his powerful arm around my waist. He lifted me up effortlessly. It happened so quickly. As I struggled, he started laughing as he carried me away from the door. He pushed me hard on to the stairs, and my head cracked off a banister rail.

He began unbuttoning his trousers and I started shaking my head. I couldn't move. I was like a rabbit caught in the headlights of a car. He forced himself on top of me, pushed his hand up my skirt and pulled my knickers to one side. The horrors of what Granddad had done to me came flooding back. I wanted to scream but I couldn't. Why must men do these things to girls? I thought. As I had done before, I found myself wondering if this act was normal, if all girls had to put up with it every so often. It had been over four years since Granddad had abused me, but I was about to be used again.

I know this may be hard to believe these days, but, at 16, I still didn't really know what sexual intercourse was. I lay on a staircase while a total stranger thrust into me violently as my head clattered off the staircase.

It was all over in two minutes as he lay panting on top of me. Then he buttoned himself up and stood over me with a vacant look. 'Go on, you can piss off now,' he said. Then he unlocked the door and opened it. I fixed my knickers, smoothed my skirt down and walked out, terrified that he would pull me back into the house and do it all over again. As I got to the door, he shouted to me that Joan would be back there later.

I went home in tears, but this time there would be no special secret like there had been with Granddad. This time I would tell my mum what had happened. But, as I walked into the kitchen and found Mum in floods of tears again, I began to have doubts about telling her. She looked up and noticed I had been crying. Then she stood up and cuddled me, obviously thinking my tears were for Granddad. I'd be selfish burdening her now with my troubles, I thought, and decided to wait until after the funeral.

The night before the funeral, I lay awake thinking about Granddad and also about what had happened in our neighbour's house. I wondered how exactly I would tell Mum and if I should tell Dad too. I pictured the scene over and over again, wondering whether I had done anything, no matter how small, to encourage him to use me as he had. There had been no violence or threats, no punches or kicks, and he'd smiled and acted normally throughout. Was I being stupid? Was I being selfish? Had it really been such a terrible two minutes? These were the thoughts I couldn't get away from, and yet, deep down, I knew what he had done had been so very wrong.

Granddad was cremated. I wasn't expecting that, as, in all the television films I'd seen about people dying, they were buried in the ground. I sat with Mum and Dad, but my brothers were deemed to be too little to attend. I sat as the curtains closed around the coffin and wondered what happened next. The girls at school had explained that to be cremated meant to be burned. Though I didn't see any flames, I still didn't want Granddad to be burned. We just got up and left and everyone cried, including me.

I couldn't tell Mum about what had happened at Joan's on the day of Granddad's funeral. I'd tell her tomorrow.

CHAPTER ELEVEN

MARRIAGE MADE IN HELL

I moved, and could not feel my limbs:
I was so light – almost
I thought that I had died in sleep,
And was a blessed ghost.

Tomorrow never came. It was easier to block out the fact that I had been attacked by another man than to bring it all back again by telling my parents. Although at the time I didn't realise exactly what this man had done to me or that he had broken the law, I knew it somehow wasn't right. Above all else, I was confused. We had no sex education at school and no real-time playground discussions about the birds and the bees, but some of my friends had started taking an interest in boys and I'd heard a few tales about men wanting sex – though I wasn't really sure what that entailed.

I so wanted to unburden my guilt to someone but the line of least resistance was simply to say nothing. The guilt factor was gnawing away at me and I played back each step, each facial expression in my mind over and over again, wondering if I'd done something to encourage that man to use me in that way.

By this time, I'd started to develop breasts and wondered if that was a kind of green light for men to do what they wanted.

And every time I played those scenes through, I brought the horror and the guilt and the confusion to the forefront of my mind. I can fully understand these girls and women who do not press charges or do not even go to the police because every interview and every detail disclosed brings the horror back to life. There were times I wanted to tell someone, but I couldn't because it would have meant having to explain how it had happened, all the gory details. I'd have been asked if it had been the first time, and if not why not, and who was the first. I was a hopeless liar and I was scared that the truth about Granddad would have come out. I just couldn't face telling my mum what her own father had done to me.

Instead, I got on with my life and pushed the incident to the back of my mind. By now, I was 16 and the conversation revolved around one thing. Boys! Every one of my friends had a boy they fancied and, quite naturally, trying to be one of the 'gang', I made a few names up as well. I pretended to my peers I was interested in boys too, when in actual fact nothing could be further from the truth.

The death of my granddad had left an emotional, guilt-filled void, and now the rape at the hands of my neighbour's son-in-law left a huge mental scar. It was no good. Whenever I even looked at a boy, I felt dirty. I was hurting so much inside, I was angry, humiliated, but most of all I felt filthy and ashamed of the normal feelings I was beginning to experience as I moved towards my 17th birthday. It was a heartache that sometimes felt like it was suffocating me.

I met my first husband by the ice rink on Shield Road where we used to hang around. My friend at the time was Susan Cattlewood. Susan was courting a lad and one day she turned up with him and his friend. It was plainly obvious that Susan had pre-planned a little matchmaking, though at the time I was too naive to realise. The thought of a relationship with a boy after all I'd been through was simply unthinkable. By now, I knew a little bit about sex and what some of my friends were getting up to behind their parents' backs, but, after all I'd been through, I couldn't imagine such acts could be pleasurable for a girl.

Susan's boyfriend introduced his mate. I won't use his real name, I'll call him simply B for Bastard. He asked me what my name was and, before I could answer, Susan had answered for me. I wish she hadn't done that, and I wish I'd never set eyes on him. He would take me to hell and back over the next 10 years.

Even at that age, B was over-confident and cocky, with a self-assured grin permanently etched on his face. I can still picture that first meeting: what he was wearing, his smile, the things he said to me and, if there is one meeting in the world that I could turn back the clock and wish it hadn't ever taken place, it would be that one. People find it strange that I don't hate my granddad for all those things he did to me but I don't. I don't hate a single thing or person on this wonderful planet but I make an exception for B. He is a horrible, nasty man and I hate the bastard with all my heart. There are times in writing this chapter that I've felt he isn't even worth the effort and the ink, but this is an autobiography and I can't pretend that the abuse and torment and degradation didn't happen.

B turned to Susan. 'Will your mate meet me tomorrow at two o clock?'

Before I had a chance to say a word, Susan jumped in and answered for me. 'Of course she will.'

I had no intention of turning up to meet B, but Susan called for me half an hour before we were due to meet them and begged me to go. Against my better judgement, I reluctantly agreed and, although a little late, they turned up and we all walked down to Wavertree Park and hung around there. He still had that cocky smile plastered on his face.

On the way back, he asked, 'Do you want to go out with me or what?'

I told him to shut up. I didn't know what to say. I had never had a proper boyfriend before and was a little bit embarrassed, though flattered because at least someone was actually paying attention to me.

B persisted and in the end I just shrugged my shoulders and said yes. That's how our courtship started and, because of all the attention he paid me, I started to like hanging around with him. We'd go round in a big gang most of the time but occasionally we'd go out on our own and I liked the feeling of having a boyfriend. We'd go to the park, and sometimes the ice rink, but sometimes we'd just stay in and watch TV.

We were out in the park one day when I began to feel sick and dizzy. B couldn't understand why I was ill and in the end just walked away while I vomited in the bushes. He made an excuse about having to meet one of his mates and told me to call him when I was better. His lack of concern and selfish attitude should have told me something.

The sickness went on and on, generally each morning, and eventually one day I collapsed in school. They took me to the first-aid room, asked me a few questions, then a teacher told me we were going to the doctor's.

I sat down and described my symptoms to the doctor; he sent me into the toilet to pee into a bottle. I didn't know what was happening, or why he asked me to do that. At 16 years of age, I did not know what caused pregnancy. I had heard the playground gossip that, if a boy kissed you, you could end up pregnant and even that you could 'catch' pregnancy from a toilet seat. One girl who came from Ireland had been told by the nuns not to sit down on a warm seat that a man had just sat on because you could get pregnant that way! Honestly, that is not a joke – the poor girl wouldn't sit on a bus seat in Liverpool for years until she found out the truth.

I returned to the doctor's a few days later and he confirmed to me that I was pregnant.

'You are having a baby, young lady,' he said and explained how it had happened and how long it would take to arrive. Only then, sitting there in the doctor's surgery, did I realise the exact time and place I had become pregnant.

What would Mum and Dad say? To make matters worse, Mum had also announced she was having a baby a few weeks before. What a bloody mess. Mum was in floods of tears when I told her and I begged her not to tell Dad.

When Dad came home for his dinner, he sent me over the road to Tom's shop for some pies and sausage rolls. When I got back, Dad was sitting on the couch with his head in his hands. I looked at Mum and her eyes were all red. Then Dad looked at the paper bag from Tom's shop and said, 'What are you having?'

'I'm having a sausage roll,' I said.

Dad leaped to his feet and shouted, 'I think you've had enough fucking sausage rolls, haven't you?'

I shook my head. 'You can have the sausage roll then,' I said. 'I'll have the pie.'

Dad's face turned red with anger. 'Whose is it?'

I looked at the bag. 'The sausage roll or the pie?'

'Whose is it?' he screamed.

'Take the sausage roll then, I'll have the pie.'

'I don't want the fucking sausage roll.'

'Well, take the pie then.'

I swear this exchange went on for a full five minutes until he mentioned a baby.

'I don't know what you're talking about, Dad.'

'Whose is it?'

By now, Mum was crying and Dad was asking who the father was. The penny dropped – I really thought he had been talking about the sausage roll.

'You'd better start telling me who got you pregnant. I'll kill the bastard.' He was pacing the room. 'I'll never be able to hold my head up around here again.'

True to form, I tried a little humour. I don't know why, it just came out. 'Why, are you pregnant as well?'

He trembled with rage. 'Who made you pregnant?'

I shook my head but didn't answer.

'You're not telling me because you don't know.' He pointed out of the window. 'Why don't you go and lie in the street and let everyone have a go?'

Fear turned to rage and everything that had ever happened to me came flooding back in an instant. 'I've been with everyone. That's how I got pregnant.'

I'd never answered Dad back like that. He looked at me in horror and smacked me right across the face. Next thing I lunged at him, and we fell to the floor fighting. Mum tried to pull us apart, shouting, 'Leave her alone, she's pregnant.'

Dad pushed me away and went into the kitchen, slamming the door behind him. There was an instant eerie silence and I could hear him sobbing his heart out. It was the most painful thing that could have happened, and he didn't deserve that.

As a result, Mum and Dad barred me from going out and I couldn't go to see B. They naturally assumed the baby was his. The word on the street filtered over to him and he eventually sneaked round to see me. He explained that the only way to see each other was to get married, and then Mum and Dad couldn't stop us from seeing each other.

'You want to marry me?' I asked incredulously.

He shrugged his shoulders. 'Why not?'

I sat on the kitchen floor with my back to the wall as B grinned at me from the kitchen table and I actually began to think it wouldn't be such a bad idea. I dreamed of a new start with my own husband, a chance to start life all over again. We'd get a council house and B would get a job and we'd live happily ever after like they did on those television programmes, and we'd have more children and a nice house with a little garden, and maybe even get a dog and have holidays and nice things out of the catalogue.

I was only 16, and needed my parents' permission, but quite naturally they were appalled at the idea. They tried to stop it by not signing the licence to allow me to marry. Eventually, I persuaded them to sign.

As Dad hovered over the form with his pen in his hand, he looked up from the table.

'Promise me one thing, Christine.'

I nodded.

'Promise me you won't make me regret this.'

I smiled and replied, 'I won't, Dad.'

Our wedding was set for Wednesday, 8 July 1975. My wedding ring was silver; I bought it myself for just £1.75, as B claimed he was 'short' until the end of the week. Dad's sister Sandra lent me her blue maxi dress, and me and Dad got the number 27 bus to the registry office. Mum couldn't make the wedding as she'd given birth to Jason a few days before and was still in hospital.

After the registry-office wedding, we moved into B's mother's house in her spare bedroom at the top of her three-storey house.

As I moved my few meagre possessions in, it dawned on me that I didn't even know what B's job was. When I asked him, he just shook his head. He eventually told me that he was unemployed but his weekly giro was more than enough and anyway he claimed he could make more money out on the street than he could in any stupid factory. I actually believed him.

The house was not exactly Buckingham Palace, but at least we had a roof over our heads and it was quite romantic because we could see the stars at night. This was because of a large hole in the ceiling. When it rained, it was like an assault course with pans and buckets all over the place to catch the drips. We huddled under the blankets and laughed our heads off like two little children. We *were* two little children but, despite everything, life seemed perfect.

For a while at least.

CHAPTER TWELVE

A NEW ARRIVAL

O sweeter than the marriage-feast,
'Tis sweeter far to me,
To walk together to the kirk
With a goodly company!

Me and B were like gypsies, we moved around so much. I remember moving into a private flat in Arundel Avenue, Wavertree, near to Penny Lane and thinking at last we had a real home. However, there was a problem with the rent after only a few weeks and then we were back to his mother's before I knew it.

B was never in, spending most of the time with his mates, but that suited me fine. I'd come to realise that he was a useless, idle bastard, more interested in his mates than his young pregnant wife. The only thing I objected to was staying under the same roof as his mother. She was nearly as bad as her son, constantly picking faults and criticising me.

The earlier promises of enough money to live on were beginning to sound a little false. B never gave me any housekeeping, just a few pounds when he felt like it. I did my best to make our accommodation nice, and to have enough food to prepare a meal for him each evening when he came home. Some nights he didn't bother to come home and strangely enough I never asked him where he had been. For some unknown reason, I didn't like to question him.

By now I was heavily pregnant. One evening I was annoyed because B asked me to go downstairs to borrow five pounds off his mother. My back ached and I had a headache.

'Why can't you go?' I asked.

He told me his mother wouldn't give him any money, but if she thought it was for me and the baby she would.

He was wrong. 'The bastard's got more money than me, tell him,' she said as she flatly refused to give me a penny and sent me away with my tail between my legs. She gave me a lecture on housekeeping and said I should manage my money more carefully. I wish!

When I got back upstairs, B was furious with me. He came up in front of me an inch or two from my face and cursed and sneered at me saying I was a useless cunt.

'It's not my fault she won't lend me the money,' I whimpered at him, cowering into the corner of the room.

He grabbed me by the throat and, as I struggled for breath, he pushed me away hard. As I fell backwards, I caught my leg on a chair and fell to the floor. I lay there in shock. I couldn't believe what he'd just done. I had to get out of there. I got to my feet and hurried towards the door.

'Where the fuck are you going?' he sneered. B rarely shouted; a threat in a low whisper and an inch from my ear was more intimidating than any shouting and he knew it.

'Fuck off, you dickhead,' I shouted as I burst into tears. 'Don't you ever do that to me again or I'm off.'

I went to walk out of the room and he lunged at me, grabbing a handful of hair. We were struggling at the top of the stairs as he pulled my hair with one hand and slapped my head with the other. It became a tug of war and, as I fought to break free, I lost my footing. I put my hands out in front of me as I grabbed desperately at handfuls of air and sailed over the top of the stairs.

I bounced down every one of the 10 steps and landed groaning in a heap at the bottom. My head ached, my arms and legs burned where they'd connected with the edge of each wooden stair, but, worst of all, I became aware of a damp sensation between my legs.

I tried to get up but couldn't and noticed the blood running down my legs. I screamed at B to help me. Within 15 minutes, an ambulance had arrived. B insisted again and again that I'd fallen down the stairs. The ambulance man informed me on the way to hospital that the fall had started my labour off. He also told me that B had refused to get in the ambulance with me. I was six months pregnant but couldn't hold the strain of the pregnancy, and so at six o'clock on a Sunday night I gave birth to a little girl. She was three pounds two ounces and was immediately taken away from me to an incubator.

B was conspicuous by his absence. I telephoned his mum to tell her the news and asked if she could tell him to come and see me. She said she'd tell him as soon as he came home, but he never came that day.

Later on, a nurse took me to see the baby. She was the tiniest thing I had ever seen, lying there with a nappy that came up to her arms and a little doll's hat on her head. I called her Paula. I was in awe that this little baby was mine, but, because she was so small and fragile, the nurse told me I couldn't hold her just yet.

B came in to see her a few days later but seemed less interested in Paula than in the tattoo he'd just had done. It was a three-inch, three-dimensional cross in blue ink with the letters R.I.P.

written across the middle. He was so proud of it and stroked at the scabs over and over again, oblivious to the beautiful baby girl just a couple of feet away from him.

After a couple of weeks, I was discharged but Paula stayed in hospital for another three weeks, where she was fed by a tube. I went to see her every day, just looking at her in the incubator.

B decided to do his fatherly bit in registering the birth. I wrote the name Paula on a piece of paper. But he registered her as Tracy. The bastard.

I don't know why he decided to call her Tracy. I never asked. Perhaps it was out of spite or wickedness, or maybe he was just making me aware that he could do as he wanted. I don't know. I was quite upset at the time but in the end my daughter seemed to suit her new name. When they eventually put her in my arms, I felt my heart melt. I said, 'Hello, little one, I've been waiting a long time to hold you.'

A few days later, Tracy was allowed to come home. I pushed her all the way in a pram that my dad had bought for six pounds from a second-hand shop. That walk home made me feel so proud and, every step of the way, I seemed to draw strength from deep inside me.

I lay awake most of the night when Tracy first came home waiting for a slight noise or a change in her breathing so that I had an excuse to jump up and take a look at her beautiful, perfectly formed face. When she did cry, it was such a low sound you hardly knew that she was crying at all.

A few weeks later, I was all excited because we moved to a council flat. I felt sure that, by having our own place, with no one else in the house, B would change his ways.

By now, I had what everyone called woman's troubles and was under a gynaecologist. They found that I hadn't been able to hold the pregnancy because I had ruptured membranes and an incompetent cervix. The examinations were awful, yet another invasion of my young defenceless body. Because the doctor was a figure of authority, I had been brought up not to question him or doubt anything he was doing. Of course, I knew he was only trying to help but to be quite honest he brought back all of the bad memories as he prodded and messed around down there. I wanted to shout out, 'Just piss off and leave me alone.'

One day, the doctor explained he had a teaching class, and he asked me if I would have any objection to some of his students looking in on a consultation. I was too afraid to even consider refusing. He started his consultation by asking me to undress. I went behind the screen and slipped on the hospital gown before lying on the bed, while the doctor put on his surgical gloves and lubricated up. I'd forgotten all about the students by the time the doctor had inserted his instrument that opened me up. But just then the door opened. Another doctor walked in with what seemed like half of Liverpool University walking behind him. It was like I was being punished all over again and they were looking down at me, some even bending down to get a better look, like it was some sort of bloody car showroom. All I could do was hear the ticking of Granddad's clock until the humiliation was over.

Somehow, I needed to be in control of my own body and my own mind. It all seemed very easy the first day I picked up a knife. It was lying on the bench top as I walked into the kitchen. It was dirty and I remember washing it as I didn't want the crumbs to go into my veins. I took the knife upstairs into the bathroom, locked the door and sat on the floor. I removed my blouse and placed it carefully on the floor. I felt in control – not happy, just in control.

I now had the choice of how and when I was going to get hurt.

I held the knife firmly in my right hand and looked down at my stomach. I was skinny as a rake, not an ounce of fat on me and my stomach was flat and white. I placed the tip of the blade into my stomach a few inches above my belly button and pushed gently. Nothing happened. The point of the blade just disappeared into my flesh but didn't break the skin. I pushed a little harder and winced in pain as it pierced the flesh. A trickle of blood collected around the blade and I gritted my teeth and dragged it across my stomach. I settled back against the wall as an overwhelming sense of relief washed over me. Cutting into my flesh was like releasing a pressure valve that was so intense inside that the pain came as a relief.

I would make sure I was all alone in the house when I cut myself. I would scream and shout. I would cry out at the man who used me, and then call out to my granddad to give me my childhood back. It was always in the bathroom, and I'd always cut myself on the parts of my body that no one could see: my stomach, the tops of my arms, my chest.

Bizarrely, the more I hurt myself, the angrier I felt, and yet still I craved that pressure-valve release, that control. Inevitably, my mother discovered my problem and I broke down and confessed to what I'd been doing. I lied, telling her I was depressed after my nan and granddad's deaths. I never told her about the attack on me at the neighbour's house, or the abuse that Granddad had carried out on me when I had been a small girl.

The doctors I saw knew nothing, it seemed. Everything resulted in a prescription. The only things that changed were the colour of the pills. Blue to yellow then back to blue. The pills were sedatives – Valium, Ativan and the like – and I suppose at the time they worked. At least they calmed me down a little, and sent me into an emotionless-like state. But after I came off each course, a few weeks would pass by and then I would begin cutting myself again.

> *Little tiny tablet,*
> *How you control my life,*
> *Little tiny tablet,*
> *That makes the wrongs so right,*
> *You make my life a dream state,*
> *With everything a blur,*
> *And when I do not have you,*
> *I feel a panic there.*

After Tracy came home, I thought things might change, and that maybe B would take some interest in the new addition to our family. I was wrong. He wasn't interested one little bit and he spent more time away from home than ever before. I spent a lot of time at Mum's swapping baby clothes and little toys. How surreal is that?

I came back home one day and B was sitting in the chair looking angry.

'Where the fuck have you been?' he demanded.

'I've been to Mum's.'

He stood up and walked over to me. 'Where have you been?'

I repeated that I'd been to Mum's.

'Where's Tracy?' he asked.

'At Mum's.'

The conversation was going nowhere. I sighed and walked through into the kitchen. He followed me and started shouting that I hadn't asked his permission to be out so long. I ignored him and sat down on the settee, picked up a paper and started to look at it pretending to read. B tore the paper from my hands and threw it into the corner of the room. I jumped up to get it and he punched me in the face. I remember thinking at the time that I had simply walked into his hand as I jumped up. I thought I'd collided with his fist accidentally. What happened next was certainly no accident. It was the battering I have described in the prologue to this book.

CHAPTER THIRTEEN

FIGHTING FOR MY LIFE

Then like a pawing horse let go,
He made a sudden bound:
It flung the blood into my head,
And fell down in a swound.

I left Tracy at Mum's for a couple of days until the swelling from B's latest brutal attack had gone down. When I collected Tracy, I told Mum I had fallen down the stairs. Excuses… always excuses.

I can't believe now that I was getting the shit kicked out of me and telling him I was sorry. By now, the beatings were happening most weeks. The more he hit me, the more I apologised. I kept saying sorry, because I thought it might make him stop hitting me.

I started having my hair cut really short, almost shaved like a skinhead so that he had nothing to hold on to when he battered me. When I had hair, he would simply take a handful and punch and punch and punch with the other hand until I lapsed into unconsciousness, so I cut it. He wore me down verbally day by day; he broke down my confidence, then my self-esteem and my self-worth. Eventually, I started to believe everything he said. I was useless, dirty, hopeless, ugly, sometimes too fat, sometimes too thin. I've read other tales about domestic violence and why women stay with someone who beats them and the reason is mostly that the man promises to change and apologises over and over again. Not B. He never apologised, not once. The reason I stayed with him was because I was frightened he'd kill me.

He'd grab me by the throat and push his right hand with the tattoo an inch from my eyes and whisper menacingly, 'See that? Look at that, you cunt. Look at it. This is the last thing you'll ever see.'

I was trapped and had nowhere to run. Dad's words when he signed for us to get married had come back to haunt me. 'Don't make me regret this, Christine.'

As time went on, B would beat me for fun. We'd be sitting on the settee together and without any warning he would backhand me across the face.

'What was that for?' I'd ask in amazement.

He'd shrug his shoulders and say he just felt like it.

Whether or not he was angry, he'd beat me. Sometimes if he was bored, he'd get up and pick up a kitchen knife. 'Get over here now,' he'd demand as he sat at the table playing with the knife. He'd make me sit at the table with my hand spread out. He'd play chicken with the knife. That's a game that used to be played out in most inner cities, normally between two young boys. The object of the game is for the person with the knife to stab between the fingers of the person with their hand on the table. He would start slowly and gently at first then gradually increase the tempo and the force of the knife. The loser would be the person who stabbed and drew blood or the person who pulled their hand away first, hence the name of the game.

In B's games of chicken, though, we didn't take turns. If I

pulled my hand away, I got battered; if I left my hand on the table, I got stabbed... always. In the end, I learned to leave my hand on the table as a stabbed knuckle or finger was far better than a five- or ten-minute beating and I prayed that the stabbing would come sooner rather than later for obvious reasons. Most of the time, it was just a nick or a scratch, but occasionally B would open up the flesh on my hand to the bare white of the bone. I still have the scars today, reminding me almost daily of the abuse I suffered at the hands of that man.

I felt as if I didn't exist. People have asked me time and time again why I didn't just open the door and go. It sounds easy to do, but the fear of an even greater horror keeps you there. You begin to live with the pain and humiliation and think to yourself things could be worse.

The only way I can describe it is to imagine you are afraid of the dark. Imagine falling asleep in daylight and when you wake up the room is in total darkness apart from a sliver of light from the open doorway. You know that all you have to do is get up and open the door and the room will be filled with life-saving light. It's that easy. But that fear paralyses you because there's a chink of light that you crave and you start thinking, 'What happens if I get up and the door slams shut before I get there. That chink of light, representing hope, is there now so why do anything to risk it disappearing completely?' That's what it was like.

I was still alive. My chink of light was Tracy, and as long as I could hold her, touch her, feed and clothe her every day I had something; I had that daylight. If B carried out his threats and killed me, the door would slam shut and I'd have nothing. Tracy was my life, my hope. He had no time for her anyway; to him she was a nuisance. Every time she cried, he would say, 'Shut that fucking thing up or I'll throw it through the fucking window.'

I'd walk the streets day and night with Tracy in the pram just to get her out of his way. For all his threats, he never hurt the children and I could accept my hidings with the logic that if he was beating me he wasn't hurting anyone else. But I began thinking that maybe I deserved the beatings. It was all mind games with him. Some days he would be in an almost pleasant mood and he'd slide up towards me without warning and whisper in my ear, 'I'm going to fucking kill you.' Then he'd walk away as if nothing had happened, make a cup of tea or switch the TV on, and I'd think, 'Did he really say that or have I imagined it?'

My life had gone from one form of abuse to another. In a mad sort of way, the beatings from B almost seemed normal, and I wasn't the only girl being battered in my circle of friends. I'd often meet people at the park or the shops and it was not uncommon to see a black eye or a split lip. Somebody even joked one day that if a girl didn't have a black eye or a split gob it meant she was single.

There were more problems with the rent so we were on the move again, this time to 61 Holmrook Road, Norris Green. By now, B was battering me for anything. My nerves were getting worse and worse. Every time he came home, I would be trembling with fear. If he didn't beat me he'd threaten me. It was almost like a game to him. He'd throw me down on the settee for the most pathetic of reasons and draw his fist back as if to start an attack. He'd show me the RIP cross and tell me he was going to batter the shit out of me. I'd be begging him to stop with my eyes screwed tightly shut waiting for the first blow. I'd lie there screaming and crying for at least a minute or two before realising it wasn't going to happen. I'd open my eyes to find him sitting in his armchair reading the *Liverpool Echo* with a smirk on his face.

From time to time, he'd disappear for two, three, four days in a row, then turn up in the middle of the night and wake me.

'Don't you want to know where I've been?' he'd ask.

If I said no he'd batter me because I didn't care and if I said yes he'd batter me for being a nosy bitch.

I was still only 19, but I had at least half a dozen front teeth missing. I had more stitches than a patchwork quilt and my self-esteem was lower than a worm's tit. And B was really starting to play with my mind. He sent me out to the shop for some cigarettes on a wet Saturday afternoon. He pointed to the clock: it read two o'clock. He said the shop would be open after dinner time closing. The shop was only five minutes away, so I hurried there, got served quickly and hurried back.

He sat tapping on his empty cigarette box, glaring at me as I walked through the door. 'Where the fuck have you been?'

'What?'

He stood up and pointed at the clock. 'Where the fuck have you been?'

The clock read four o'clock. I stared at it in disbelief.

'Tell me where you've been, you cunt.'

I couldn't answer. I'd been away for no more than 20 minutes but the clock told me I'd been gone for two hours. I was trembling as he walked towards me and I held out the packet of cigarettes as if it would calm him down. He knocked them out of my hand and battered me senseless as I curled up into the familiar hedgehog ball, covering my head with my hands.

When he'd finished, I lay sobbing gently for 15 minutes; he kicked me two or three times for snivelling. As I dried my eyes and opened them, he was sitting in his armchair smoking a cigarette and reading the paper. I thought about my visit to the shop and went over each step wondering where I had lost the time. I was going out of my mind, losing my sanity. Only some weeks later, in a fit of laughter, did he tell me he'd put the hands on the clock forward, for a laugh.

Why do men beat their wives? It's a question I've been asked many times. I may be wrong but my overall assessment boils down to a lack of education, a throwback to Neanderthal man, the caveman. A few thousand years ago, it was a common occurrence to kill or hurt and dominate. It was human nature, I suppose. However, the human race has moved on. In the last millennium or two, man has changed, with access to books and television and the internet. Man has learned to respect others and negotiate, man can communicate, and man can study and learn about human nature and feelings. Anyone with half a brain realises that battering the shit out of a woman is probably not the best type of action to make for a successful, fulfilling and satisfying marriage.

Sadly, B's brain was the size of an undernourished pea.

It was only Tracy that kept me going. Tracy, you have always been my strength, I love you more than you could ever imagine. When you were born, I was a child with a child and I wanted a manual that would tell me how to be a good mother. Sadly, it never arrived. Some things you get wrong, sometimes more than once, and I made some big mistakes along the way for which I can only apologise. All I can say is that they were honest mistakes. Life is not a blackboard that, when you write on it and make a mistake, you can rub it out and start over again. I wish it were.

You were there through the worst years of my life and I managed to pull courage and strength from deep inside your beautiful body. When my energy was drained, you rejuvenated me. You were my strength and I love you, my beautiful baby girl, from the bottom of my heart.

By now, B was spending some time away at Her Majesty's pleasure. He was into a little petty thieving but, unfortunately for him, didn't have the brains to get away with it. His time inside ranged from 28 days to a few months. It was heaven when he was away and I enjoyed every minute of it. I played the dutiful wife and visited him when I could, but, on his very first day of freedom, he'd batter me senseless, accusing me of sleeping with his mates. I wouldn't have slept with any of them, not even under anaesthetic.

My sex life with B was almost non-existent. The expression once in a blue moon comes to mind. Yet, incredibly, at 21, I found out I was pregnant again. I was worried because by this time I was on tablets for depression, as prescribed by the doctor. The tablets only numbed my brain. I was like a heavyweight boxer going at least 10 rounds every week of my life. I had not even thought about being pregnant because I already had four miscarriages behind me as a result of the abuse. Essentially, B had beaten our four babies to death and I hated him with a passion.

Because of my medical history, the hospital suggested that I should have a stitch on the neck of the womb to try to let the pregnancy run its full course. Seven months later, I gave birth to Hayley and I had a feeling perhaps things were going to change on the home front.

Things did change: B got worse. He beat me almost every day. Even when I came in with things for the girls he would accuse me of wasting money and would hit me. Of course, they were essential things I was bringing home – food, clothes or shoes – but it made no difference. B controlled the money and always left me short, and when he came in, if there wasn't anything to eat, I would get battered again.

I went round to Mum's one day begging for some potatoes to make corned-beef hash. Mum didn't have any either but gave me a packet of Yeoman's Smash. 'You just add water,' she said, 'and you have perfect mashed potato.'

She was right: the corned-beef hash looked lovely in the Pyrex bowl with the light fluffy potato sitting on top. At least B couldn't batter me for having nothing on the table.

He was in a foul mood when he came in. He looked at the dish on the table.

'I want fritters,' he said.

I shrugged my shoulders. I wasn't the greatest cook in the world but was quite pleased with my effort.

'What's wrong with that?' I asked.

'I want fuckin' fritters.'

'I don't know how to make fritters.'

He called me a useless bastard, backhanded me and pushed me out of the way. He took the chip pan out of the cupboard and switched the cooker on. He reached into the Pyrex bowl, took a large fistful of the mixture and began pressing and kneading it into a ball. He then took a milk bottle and rolled the mixture out so it was about an inch thick. He kept looking across at me with a smug grin on his face. Within a few minutes, he'd finished and five perfectly formed fritter shapes sat on the table.

'Can't make fuckin' fritters,' he sneered. 'A fuckin' five-year-old is better in the kitchen than you are.'

As he lowered them carefully into the pan, he told me how hungry he was.

We both stood in the kitchen as the fritters cooked. B looked at his watch. After about 10 minutes, he lifted the basket to check on the progress of the fritters.

The basket was empty.

'What the fuck...?'

He looked at me then back to the pan as if they would miraculously reappear. The Smash had simply disintegrated and the corned beef had fried away to nothing. The silly bastard hadn't known they were made of Smash.

It was the funniest comedy sketch of the year. I wanted to burst out laughing. I wanted to roll around the floor holding my aching sides. Now he would go to bed hungry. B looked back at the pan with that dopey, puzzled look on his face then back at me. I shrugged my shoulders and he caught a fleeting grin on my face. He battered me with the basket two or three times and, as I fell to the floor, he left the room. I put my hand over my mouth and lay laughing in silence. How I managed to keep quiet I'll never know. The look on his face as he looked at the empty basket was just priceless.

Such moments of humour in my life were few and far between. My life was well and truly messed up. I had to find a way to get out of this situation but I was feeling both mentally and physically exhausted and close to the point of no return, close to that thin line where sanity ends and insanity begins. My brain had to take a rest, and I had to stop thinking. I was convinced that B could read my mind. I was like a robot; he controlled everything I did, and every minute of my day.

When he was out, I used to burst into tears regularly. Some days I didn't even know what I was crying for. If I cried when he was in, he beat me. I learned to stop crying, stopped feeling the pain, and I even stopped caring about what he was doing to me.

I started cutting myself again. This was something I could control. I couldn't control the beatings from B, but by cutting into my flesh *I* was the one in charge. I had made a real effort to stop cutting myself when Hayley was born. Now, with two daughters, I had double the reason to live, but I was afraid that they would hate me because of the type of environment I was bringing them up in. I had nothing, and nor did my beautiful girls. Anything not fixed to the floor B sold to one of his cronies. He only left me with tat... junk... rubbish.

I had a cooker that should have been condemned – it didn't even have a handle on it, and every time I used it I had to open it with pliers. I hired my washing machine for two pounds a week, and I had an old-fashioned record player without a lid that I'd bought from a jumble sale for a pound. My dad gave me LPs to play on it, but, if he ever gave me a half-decent record, B would sell it.

In my eight-year marriage, I only managed to save up enough money for one thing. I'd been to my auntie Sandra's and was admiring a smoked-glass table and four black patent leather chairs with stainless-steel silver legs. She told me she was going to sell it as she was getting a new one. Back home, we had nothing to eat our dinner from and I dreamed of putting some plates on to a table so we could sit down and eat properly, like real people did. Auntie Sandra said she would sell it for five pounds. Five pounds was a lot of money back then and it took me nearly a month scrimping and scraping to pull that fiver together. I was so proud when Hayley, Tracy and me sat down to our first dinner.

By now, B was in and out of jail on a regular basis. When he wasn't in jail, he would spend days away from the house. Every time he turned up, he found some excuse to give me a hiding. I feared for my life every time he was around. I'd do anything he said double quick just to try to keep him happy. I could write another six chapters detailing the abuse but this book would never get finished. A few incidents, however, always spring to mind.

My mum gave me an old iron as Dad had bought her a new one. For once, B decided to lend a hand and put a plug on it for me. While he was putting it on with an old knife, he asked me to make a cup of tea. For once everything seemed normal to me. He hadn't demanded a cup of tea, he'd asked, and he was even playing the doting husband putting a plug on the iron just to help me. I stood by the pan of hot water waiting for it to boil, as I didn't have a kettle.

B began to get impatient: 'Where's the fuckin' tea, fat arse?'

Fat arse: that was a laugh. I weighed six stone wet through because there was never any money for food. I skipped at least one meal a day just to try to feed my daughters. Living with B was the best diet in the world.

'Hurry up. Where the fuck is it?'

I looked at the pan and begged it to boil faster as he became more and more agitated.

By the time I carried his tea through, I was trembling with fear. As I leaned over to place it on the table, a few drops spilled on to his trousers. It wasn't enough tea to scald an ant but he jumped up screaming as if he'd had a ton of molten lead poured on to him. His reaction was to plunge the knife into my leg. The knife missed my kneecap and stuck fast in the ligaments that hold the kneecap to the shin bone. The pain was indescribable. I expected the knife to fall to the floor but it just stuck fast. No blood, nothing. It was almost surreal. The blood came as I pulled the knife from my knee and dropped it on to the floor. B casually picked it up and finished assembling the plug while I limped away to look for a bandage.

Another time, I had washed his trousers and a pound note

fell out of his pocket when I was hanging them out to dry. The pound note was soaking and I began to panic. The poor Queen looked like John Merrick, so I decided to iron it dry before he came in. He walked in a few seconds before I was finished and caught me in the act. I looked up and said I'd found the money in his pocket and tried to explain why the note was wet. It made no difference. He called me a thieving bastard and punched me to the floor. He kicked at my curled-up shape until he was out of breath. Needless to say, I never laundered money again.

During our eight years of marriage, B kicked me and punched me, headbutted and bit me, stabbed me and even burned me with cigarettes. Any form of physical violence you can think of, he used against me. But the worst attack of all would leave me fighting for my life.

CHAPTER FOURTEEN

MY DARKEST HOUR

How long in that same fit I lay,
I have not to declare;
But ere my living life returned,
I heard, and in my soul discerned
Two voices in the air.

One beating stands out from all the others, a beating when he nearly killed me.

B came in with two of his cronies. They had all been to the pub and called into the chip shop on the way home. I was sitting on the sofa as he walked through the door.

'Hey, cunt, get off that seat and give me mates a seat.' He cuffed me across the back of the head. 'Get on the floor like the dog you are.'

My inside was churning. As I sat down as instructed, he kicked me in the back.

'Don't just sit there, you lazy get, go and get us some plates.'

Like a robot I jumped up and got them. His pathetic mates were grinning like imbeciles. When I gave him the plates, he pointed to the floor.

'Sit... now!'

I sat on the floor like an obedient little lapdog waiting for its next command.

I sat for an hour not daring to move while they watched the film *Bonnie and Clyde*. My stomach was churning – I knew it was only a matter of time. His two mates made their excuses and left. B showed them to the door. When he came back in, he scraped what they had left on to one plate and turned to face me.

'This is yours,' he said. 'Eat it like a dog.'

He put it on the floor. It was disgusting: a mixture of cold fish skins, chips and curry sauce and the crust of a greasy mince pie.

'I don't want it,' I said quietly.

'Eat the fucker now.'

'But I'm not hungry.'

'On your hands and knees now.'

I stood up to clear the plates. He came towards me with the plate piled high.

I tried to stand tall and he looked me right in the face.

'So you don't want it then.'

'No thanks,' I whispered. I could feel my legs shaking.

'What's that? No? I can't hear what you're saying.'

I shook my head. He stood and sneered and he looked at the white china plate piled high with the leftovers. Without warning, he smashed the plate into my face. The plate broke into three or four pieces with the force of the impact and I wondered what damage it had done to my face. The sheer power and effort he'd put into it had taken him and me over the back of the settee. I thought I'd broken my back and lay groaning in a heap. The food was in my mouth, up my nose, in my hair and in my eyes. I struggled to see, I struggled to breathe. I was convinced I was going to die. This wasn't a case of rubbing some food in my face. He'd hit me hard enough to smash the plate and kill me. Any one of those broken pieces of crockery could have caused serious damage.

He wasn't finished with me. He wiped the food from my eyes and showed me the crucifix tattoo.

'Remember?' he said. 'The last thing you'll ever see, bitch.'

'Please,' I begged, 'I can't breathe.'

He took a hold of my hair and dragged me down the hallway like a cavewoman, kicking me every two or three steps. I begged for mercy as he dragged me into the kitchen.

'I can't breathe.'

I was on the verge of unconsciousness as I heard him turning on the taps and wondered what he was up to. For a second, I thought he was filling the sink up to wash the food and blood off my face.

I was wrong. He was filling the sink up to drown me.

He dragged me up by my hair and plunged my face into the water. He held it there for what seemed like forever as the cold water cascaded over my head. I struggled and gasped for breath as water filled my nose, mouth and throat and seeped deep into my lungs. Then I stopped and became aware of an inner calm. It was no use struggling. What sort of life was I fighting for anyway?

As I gave up, the stiffness in my body disappeared. I flopped forward and took a deep breath as the water flowed into my lungs. B sensed the change in my body and let go. I fell to the floor. For a second or two, I lay still, wanting to die, wanting to fall asleep and never wake up. But then my stomach and lungs kicked into survival mode and I spewed the water and regurgitated food all over the kitchen floor. B kicked me in the stomach for making a mess, then picked up his coat and left.

It was as much as I could take. I crawled towards the broken pieces of crockery and picked out the longest sharpest piece. I gripped it hard and placed it on my wrist. I held my breath, closed my eyes and pulled. I opened my eyes briefly to see the deep-red arterial blood spurt into the air, then closed my eyes and drifted away.

I awoke to find my next-door neighbour standing over me. My neighbour said she had heard the commotion and had arrived a few minutes after I'd slashed my wrist. If she'd arrived five minutes later, I would have died. I'd made a good job of the wrist, and my fingers were cut to ribbons where I'd held the piece of plate. This wasn't a cry for help; I had wanted to die. Incredibly, even after this incident, I still refused my neighbour's advice to call the police, fearing an even worse fate if they got involved.

I stayed away from Mum's for almost two weeks until the swelling had gone down and the bruising had disappeared. I felt awful about not going to see her, especially as some months earlier Mum had suffered a stroke which had left her paralysed down one side and she was very, very frail. My visits with the girls always perked her up and I tried to visit her most days, but, at this particular time, I couldn't turn up in the state I was in. During this long absence, she must have wondered what she'd done to upset me. B was now beginning to affect the quality of her life too.

'I missed you terrible,' she said when I finally turned up, fairly confident that everything had healed just enough for her not to notice. I made sure I had covered up the scar on my left wrist. Tracy was at school by this time, but Mum was over the moon to see Hayley and fussed around her like the mother hen that she was. After a while, I asked if she could look after Hayley while I nipped down to the shops. I left them playing a game of Snap on the kitchen table. I had been away no longer than an hour, but I knew something was wrong when I noticed Mum crying on the settee while Hayley stroked her hair and tried to comfort her.

Mum explained that B had come looking for me while I was at the shops. He'd barged into the house demanding to speak to me and had pushed her over, accusing her of hiding me. She may have had a bad heart and been semi-paralysed, but he still dared to push my mother over! Mum wasn't hurt but it was clear she was in shock.

I was seething with anger. That's how it had started with me: a push, then a shove and then a slap and a fist. My head was in turmoil and I wanted to hurt this bastard badly. Mum explained through the tears that he'd had another girl in tow. Mum explained how the girl had laughed as B had pushed her to the floor. Bastard. Bastard. Bastard.

I left Hayley with Mum and stormed out of the house. One of his friends lived in a flat five minutes' walk away. He spent more time there than he did at home. That's where he would be, and I was going to hurt him just as soon as I caught up with him.

I don't know where I found the courage from but I wasn't going to crawl away and hide any longer. I could accept my beatings and had learned to live with them, but now he'd started on my mother. All I could picture was Mum's face twisted in anguish as the tears rolled down her cheeks.

On the way to his mate's flat, I passed a bin that had an old stiletto shoe sticking out of the rubbish. I picked it up, shook a piece of stale lettuce from it and slipped it in my bag.

When I got to the flat, his mate answered the door and, to my disappointment, told me B had been and gone. I turned to walk away when his mate let slip that B had said he would be coming back soon.

'He owes me a few quid,' the mate said. 'He promised he'd let me have it today.'

I walked up the flight of stairs that led to the next landing and sat down. I took the stiletto from my bag and held it in my hand. It took B and his girlfriend nearly two hours to arrive. I had thought that my anger might have subsided by then.

It hadn't. I heard him knock on the door and the sound of his voice as he made some sort of clever quip to the girl. Then I launched myself from the stairs above him. I'd buried the stiletto half an inch into his skull before he even knew what was happening. I pulled it out and hit him another two times before the girl managed to get between us begging me to stop. I turned on her. She had stood by laughing while B had pushed my mother to the floor. I punched her twice in the face, cracked her with the stiletto and grabbed a handful of her hair calling her all the names under the sun for laughing at my poor defenceless mother.

I had a vision of my mother lying on the floor. By now, B had recovered and tried to pull me off her. What a hero, a knight in shining armour. He pushed me up against the wall and drew back his fist to hit me. I struck out with my foot and caught him between the legs with a well-timed kick. With B crumpled in a heap, I hit the girl twice more, and then kicked B twice in the stomach. I am not ashamed to admit I was like a woman possessed: a total maniac. The three of us fought for at least two or three minutes and eventually the odds against me told. B landed two punches and I hit the floor. I leaped back up and spat at him, 'Is that the best you can do?'

I went for the girl again as B battered me to the bottom.

'Is that your best shot, you fucking wimp?' I screamed, launching myself at him again with both fists flailing.

B's punches were weak now and his girlfriend had backed away into the corner of the passageway in submission. Her hands were held high, like a gunfighter in surrender mode.

B's eyes were different now, different to any eyes I had ever seen before. The cockiness behind them had gone. Now I stared into the eyes of a worried man, a man who only liked to hit people that didn't hit back.

By the time his friend interrupted the proceedings and gripped me in a bear hug, B had backed into the same corner as his girlfriend and was simply trying to defend himself from the punches I was raining down on him.

He was a beaten man and I had turned a huge corner. This man would never control me again and I would take any steps necessary to get him out of my life forever.

B didn't come home for a few days and when he did he acted as if the fight had never taken place. I plucked up the courage to announce I would be divorcing him. I half-expected him to leap up from the settee and batter me. He never moved a muscle.

A few weeks later, I got a visit from the local police saying B had been locked up for robbery and could I get down to Bridewell Street police station to stand surety for him.

'What does surety mean?' I asked the desk sergeant when I got there.

He explained that, as long as I signed the surety form, B would get bail and be allowed out. Surety meant that I was responsible for him and, if he absconded, in effect I would get the blame.

'So I just have to sign for him and he's free?'

The policeman nodded.

'What's he been charged with?' I asked.

The policeman smiled; he was going to enjoy the next bit. He was about to disclose that B had another 'friend'. To the copper, people like B were vermin, filth, something you scraped off the sole of your shoe. He was right; that described

B to a T. And of course the police simply assumed that the wives and girlfriends of vermin like that were tarred with the same brush. After all, here I was doing my duty for my husband, ready to stand surety for him. In the eyes of the law, and this copper in particular, we were as bad as each other.

The desk sergeant told me that B had a girlfriend and she had accused him of robbing her. It was a different girlfriend to the one I had beaten up a few weeks before. B claimed he was only taking back what he had bought for her children. I couldn't believe it. I couldn't believe he was seeing someone else but more upsetting than that was the fact he'd been spending money on her and her children. I began to wonder if it were true and if he'd actually bought things for her children. Was that where all the money had gone? He'd never bought Tracy or Hayley as much as a penny chew, a birthday or Christmas present, and he'd kept them hungry and short of clothes and shoes the whole of their short lives. An overwhelming hatred consumed me.

The desk sergeant interrupted my train of thought. 'You can see him now. You can sign the form on the way out.'

They took me downstairs to an interview room and B was sitting at a table with two policemen standing either side of him.

'Where the fuck have you been?' he snarled. 'Get me the fuck outa here.'

I was stunned and shocked by the revelations upstairs. I wondered what sort of time in jail he would get if he was found guilty.

'Aren't you fuckin' listenin' to me, you cunt? Get me out of here now.'

The two coppers had seen it all before. They looked genuinely sorry for me… they pitied me. *I* pitied me, married to such a low-life specimen. I looked him in the eyes and half-expected him to start drooling at the mouth, such was his contempt towards me, and yet standing in front of him was his saviour, his get-out-of-jail-free card.

'Get the fuckin' paper signed, you cunt, just as quick as you like.'

B had a short memory; he had forgotten how I had stood up to him only a few days before.

He rose to his feet. 'Aren't you fuckin' listening?'

I grinned and shook my head. 'Not really.'

'What?'

He stood in stunned silence for a few brief seconds, unable to come to terms with what he'd heard.

'Have you signed it?'

I shook my head again.

'Sign the fuckin' thing then and let me come home.'

I leaned forward. 'I'm not signing it.'

B couldn't believe what he had just heard. 'What did you say?'

'Get used to the bars on the windows. I'm signing nothing.'

B sprang towards me but I didn't move an inch. The two coppers bundled him back into his seat.

The desk sergeant turned to face me and I swear I caught the faint trace of a smile. 'You realise what this means?'

I smiled. 'Yes, he stays in jail until the trial.'

'Yes. You're sure that's what you want?'

I turned and walked towards the door. 'I've never been so sure of anything in my life,' I replied.

As I reached the door, I turned round and faced him. I walked back to the table and took off my wedding ring. I placed it in the middle and told him it was over.

'You'll hear from my lawyer in due course,' I said. 'I want you out of my life forever.'

B got 18 months in prison and I never visited him once despite numerous telephone calls from him and his mother. Each day that passed without him, I grew in strength knowing I wasn't going to take him back. At one point, he barricaded himself into his cell demanding to see his wife, believing the authorities were preventing me from going in. He was that stupid!

The governor must have taken great pleasure in telling him the truth. I plucked up the courage to start divorce proceedings against him by posting the necessary paperwork to him in jail. True to form, he sent everything back unsigned and ripped up. Half of me expected him to take the hint that I no longer wanted anything to do with him and would find somewhere else to live on his release.

I was wrong, though. After he'd served his sentence, he turned up at my door all guns blazing and threatening to kill me. I'd changed the locks and refused to let him in.

He was punching and kicking at the door. 'I'm gonna fucking kill you,' he bellowed through the letter box. Tracy and Hayley were crying by now, wondering who this monster was at the door.

I telephoned the police, and, shortly after, two huge policemen turned up as he was making inroads into the frame of the door. B was lucky that door frame held – I was standing behind it with a six-inch kitchen knife and part of me wanted the frame to give. Make no mistake, had that happened, I would have plunged that knife right into his heart, up to the hilt.

As I spotted the police, I returned the knife to the kitchen and calmly walked back and opened the door. The police took me through to the kitchen and asked what the problem was. I explained what I had been through and his history of violence against me. B ranted on and on, denying he'd ever laid a hand on me. I kept shouting at him to get out of my house.

'If I hit her, where are all the marks?' he shouted at one of the policemen.

The bigger copper walked over to him menacingly so that he was an inch away from his face. I just about managed to hear what he said. The copper said he could quite easily beat him to within an inch of his life and there wouldn't be a single mark on his body.

B nearly shit himself and for the second time I saw him as the coward he was. The copper stayed in his face, daring B to make a move or say something out of order. Both me and the copper so wished he'd reacted but he didn't. B cowered in the corner trembling, unable to utter one word. Only when the copper moved away did he find his voice again. The spineless bastard.

I told the police I wanted him out of my house but B refused to go, claiming it was his name on the rent book. The older policeman took me to one side.

'There's nothing we can do, love. He hasn't hit you and it is his house if his name's on the rent book.'

'He was kicking the door in.'

'It's his door.'

B was now looking smug. 'It's my fuckin' house and I'm going nowhere.'

I felt my strength beginning to sap again just sitting in the same room as him. I'd had months building myself up and knew I was stronger than him. I made the decision there and then. It was only four walls and a roof, sparsely furnished and tatty. Why was I wasting my energy to fight to stay here? Even if I managed to persuade the police to throw him out this time, B could find me any time he wanted. It wasn't that I was frightened of him any more; those days were over. But I knew that, every time he turned up at the door, he would bring me down and drain me of my newfound energy. So I was leaving.

I took Tracy and Hayley to the front door and told them to play in the garden. I walked back in and told the policemen I was going. B looked a little surprised. The older policeman smiled. I tried to put a few meagre possessions into a bag, but every time I picked something up B screamed at the police that he'd bought it and I was stealing.

'That's mine,' he'd shout. 'She's taking that nowhere.'

'I want the kids' clothes,' I said.

B jumped up. 'I'll get them for you. Good fuckin' riddance, fuck off and don't ever come back.'

As he left the room, I looked over at my pride and joy, my smoked-glass table that had come from Auntie Sandra, the only thing that I'd managed to buy and keep in eight years of marriage. The only reason he hadn't sold it was because he had been in jail.

'That's mine,' I said to the policemen. 'I bought that, it's mine, and I want it.'

The policemen looked at each other. One of them said, 'We can hardly get that in the panda car, love, can we?'

B came back with a small pile of the girls' clothes. He was smiling. I looked down at the clothes. They were rags, he'd ripped them to shreds while he was upstairs, and now I knew why it had taken him so long. The bastard had sat in the bedroom with a knife or a pair of scissors and shredded my daughters' clothes to bits. That incident alone sums up the man.

One of the coppers took a step towards him and for a second I thought he was going to belt him. He scuttled away like the sewer rat that he was and sat at the table grinning. He sat at the table… *my* table.

The older copper put an arm round me. 'C'mon, love, go, leave him.'

I nodded my head. 'OK, I just need to get one last thing.'

'Good, go and get it then.'

I could feel B's eyes penetrating the back of my neck as I walked over to the cupboard under the stairs where he kept his tools. I stretched into the blackness and felt for his hammer. I found it and closed my hand round the wooden shaft. I held it by my side shielding it from the view of the police as I walked back. As I got near the table, I broke into a run and raised the hammer above my head. B curled up into a ball expecting a cracked skull. Amazingly, the two policemen just stood and watched. I brought the hammer crashing down through the top of the glass table. It shattered into a thousand shards.

I walked out with my head held high. There was no way I was going to leave that table with him.

CHAPTER FIFTEEN

WALKING AWAY

There passed a weary time. Each throat
Was parched, and glazed each eye.
A weary time! a weary time!
How glazed each weary eye –,
When looking westward, I beheld
A something in the sky.

I walked out on B on 17 December 1982, leaving behind everything I owned. In essence I wasn't walking away from very much – my worth amounted to a few pots and pans, half a set of crockery and a few sticks of furniture begged, stolen or borrowed. I had no jewellery, not even a watch. I walked away with just the clothes I was wearing, and the same went for Tracy and Hayley. To make matter worse, Christmas was only a few days away.

We spent our first few days with Mum and Dad. They never asked why I had left B but I'm convinced they knew the reason. I had slipped or fallen down too many flights of stairs than was physically possible and, each time I announced my latest accident, Mum would give me a strange look of mother's intuition.

I moved into a council house in Croxdale Road, Huyton, on 21 December. It was unfurnished and I only had a few pounds in my purse, but, worse, it was fire-damaged and had no electric. The council explained that I would have to move in before they could carry out the necessary repairs and switch the electric on. So I had no option on that Tuesday but to move into that cold, dark house. I prepared the children for the darkness ahead by pretending it was just a big game, an adventure in a derelict house like the ones I'd enjoyed in childhood with Brian.

With no cooker, I couldn't cook anything, and made a plateful of cheese sandwiches for my daughters' tea. Fortunately, Sue Ashton, my social worker at the time, had told me she would call round when we were settled in. With her husband Alan, she turned up with fish and chips and a big bottle of cream soda fizzy pop. They were the best fish and chips I'd ever tasted. While we ate, Alan rigged up a car battery and a headlight which he hung from the light fitting in the lounge. It was a massively generous gesture by Sue and Alan who had every right to be preparing for their own family Christmas.

I am all too aware of the filth and vermin that walk Britain's streets and of the low-lifes who in my opinion don't deserve to live within a civilised society. But, even when my confidence in the human race is at rock bottom, people like Sue and Alan Ashton appear to restore my faith.

Other friends and family members rallied round. I was given an old sofa, a table and chairs, and just enough kitchen utensils for me to prepare and cook a meal. There was even someone – who, God forgive me, I now can't remember – who had given me a black and white portable TV.

With no violence or arguments, Christmas 1982 was my best since childhood. I had peace of mind and was learning to start smiling again. I'm actually convinced my girls noticed the change in me and so they too seemed so much happier. We had each other.

A turkey dinner was out of the question; we had chips and egg for our Christmas dinner. The girls woke up to two presents each, which Santa had just about managed to find. Tracy had a small vanity case with a yellow plastic umbrella strapped to the side and Hayley had a little teddy bear with shiny glass eyes. Sue Ashton had also bought them a big tube of Smarties each. They played with their presents for hours.

For me, that Christmas marked a new start in life, and a time to reflect. I didn't have a pot to piss in, or a window to throw it out of, but I was having the best night's sleep I could ever have imagined. B was gone and nothing he could do would make me afraid of him any more. This newfound peace helped me to find a new me. Having nothing was worth everything.

Croxdale Road, where we now lived, is situated in the last part of Liverpool before it drifts into the Dovecote area of Huyton. The community that lived around us would become invaluable. A few days after I moved in, the woman from next door introduced herself. Her name was Crissy Atkinson, and she inspired my stage name because she was such a lovely, kind, wise woman. She may have long since passed away, but I will never forget her. Next door to Crissy lived a woman called Margie Jones, and little did I know then that she would eventually become like the sister I never had. Across from our house lived a woman called Gerry and her husband Deemo Povey, a couple who always treated me like part of their extended family. Lastly, around the corner lived Gill and Tony Gustafson. I need to name these people because they were the main foundation stones that enabled me to turn my life back around. All are lifelong friends, and all hold a special place in my heart.

Apart from my two beautiful daughters, my marriage had been a disaster. I had been the punchbag and a football for a sadist. I was more convinced than ever that B had actually enjoyed every beating he gave me. He had given me a broken nose, fractured my skull, and, as I went over my numerous trips to the doctors and hospital, I counted up that I'd had over 60 stitches to hold my face and head together. I couldn't quite believe that it had taken me eight years to come to my senses.

I was persuading myself that I was becoming stronger, but I had to admit that he was still in my waking thoughts, appearing like a devil in my head every time I opened my eyes. I felt it was only a matter of time before he found me, or before I would meet him in the street. I wondered what his reaction might be. Meanwhile, I gained strength from my daughters, my family and my wonderful new neighbours, and grew more and more certain that he could never torment me again. I'd sit and talk with Margie in particular and she'd sit there like a counsellor, listening and giving advice on how to banish my demons.

The fear was disappearing, and, like a bird, I felt free and ready to soar. At face value, my benefit money was not a fortune and of course I still had to be very careful, but for the first few weeks I felt like a millionaire. B had never allowed me to cash the weekly giro and gave me no more than a few pounds each week. And now here I was in control of my own money. I can't remember the exact amount of my weekly benefit but it was more than enough and I could even afford to buy new clothes for Hayley and Tracy instead of relying on hand-me-downs and charity shops.

I would get my money on a Monday and buy three bus zone tickets. I took the girls into Liverpool and on nice days we would go to Southport beach. To the others sitting on that bus, it was just part of everyday life and normal.

Not for me. Sitting on a bus with my two girls, and not having to worry about anything other than the weather was the greatest freedom in the world and something very, very special. I would pack a plastic bag with crab-paste butties (because they were only 15p a jar and the meat ones were 25p), a packet of custard creams or fig rolls, two packets of crisps and a bottle of lemonade. A feast, and at a grand total cost of… about 65p.

At Southport beach, I'd spend all day watching the girls play by the sea, watching their happy smiling faces as they tucked into their 65p banquet, knowing that when I got back home in the evening it was just me and them. No hostility, no anger, no violence. A normal home: something that had been denied to all of us for such a long time.

Of course, there were some bad times too, occasions where I hardly had a penny in my purse. How do you tell your kids there is no food? But we survived. I'd go shopping at somewhere like the Co-op, I'd have no more than a couple of quid and buy the essentials like milk and bread, tins of beans and packets of cereal. As we walked around the shop, I'd open a pack of sausage rolls and give them to Hayley and Tracy and tell them to eat. When they were finished, I'd find them a pie; once I remember them demolishing a pack of ham between them and then finishing off with two KitKats. Needless to say, I never paid for them. I convinced myself that it wasn't stealing, it was survival: a mother making sure her cubs' bellies were at least half-full.

Sue Ashton delivered some bad news after the New Year. She said B had been to the authorities demanding to see Hayley and Tracy. He claimed I was preventing him from seeing them.

Thankfully, B was cooperating in divorce proceedings, realising that there was no going back. Sue advised me that it would get very complicated and messy if I refused to allow him to see the girls and, because he had agreed to the divorce, it was better in the long run if he was allowed access. Far better to allow him access, she suggested, than to go down the custody route. She frightened the life out of me when she mentioned custody of the children. Even if it was a million-to-one shot that he would win custody, it was not a chance I was willing to take. I therefore agreed to allow him access. I did, however, take out an injunction against him on Sue's advice.

I had to meet up with him sooner or later and so I asked Sue to accompany me on a pre-arranged visit to Holmrook Road. He was in a foul temper when we arrived but I had prepared myself mentally to face up to him yet again. He was sitting on the settee smoking, while the carcass of the broken table I had smashed was still lying in the middle of the living room.

B kept going on about wanting to see his girls. What a complete joke! He'd had no time for them when they were living under the same roof as him and yet here he was playing the aggrieved father. B cursed and swore throughout the meeting and Sue Ashton looked terrified. He stood up and began pacing back and forward just a few feet from me. As he came close to me, my skin crawled and I wondered how I had shared a house and a bed with this man for so long. Sue was doing all the talking and casually notified B that I had an injunction on him. B walked over towards Sue and asked what an injunction was. As Sue explained, he walked over to me. He turned back to Sue, and growled, 'An injunction? She's gonna fuckin' need an injunction.'

B caught me by surprise as he powered his fist into my face.

I had no chance to recover and as I slumped to the floor he was on me like a hyena, punching me unconscious.

Afterwards, Sue explained how she tried to pull him off but he'd just thrown her away. It should be the requisite of a social worker to be at least six feet tall and a minimum of 12 stone. Unfortunately, Sue wasn't quite built for fighting. She later explained how B had kicked at my unconscious body until he was breathless. In tears, she told me she thought he'd killed me.

I had been taken to Walton Hospital with a suspected fractured skull and Sue was there when I regained consciousness. I was annoyed that I hadn't seen the attack coming. Later, when I had to talk to B on the telephone, I called him the coward that he was. I said that I'd never sit down in his company again and anything he wanted to try with me I would be ready for. And I was. Every time I met B thereafter, I prepared myself for the fight that I knew I would win. I never turned my back on him or gave him the chance to spring a surprise.

My divorce took a long time and he tried to intimidate me throughout but not once did I waver or give in to him. He now had access to Hayley and Tracy and there was nothing I could do to prevent him knowing where I was living. He'd telephone me and arrange a time when he could come and collect them and I'd get them ready. He'd promise them a trip to the beach or into town, sometimes just a trip to the local park. Tracy and Hayley would get all excited and talk about nothing else for hours before he was due to arrive. But he rarely turned up, leaving the girls bitterly disappointed. One day, he rang up and announced a weekend trip to New Brighton. Tracy listened in to the conversation and as I replaced the receiver she burst into tears. She sobbed as she told me she didn't want to see Daddy any more as he didn't love her and never came when he promised.

The following day, Tracy was still adamant she didn't want to see him, and I telephoned B trying to explain that he'd let them down so often it was an inevitable reaction. Of course, he blamed me for poisoning the girls' minds and his last words before he slammed down the phone was that no one would stop him seeing his kids.

I was in the kitchen peeling some potatoes when I heard a knock at the front door. I walked through to the hallway. B stood menacingly in front of me red with rage. He was shouting at Tracy.

'What's this about you not wanting to see me?'

Tracy was terrified and bolted past me up the stairs.

'No one's gonna stop me from seeing those fucking kids.'

'Get out now,' I shouted at him.

We both looked up to the top of the stairs at the same time. Tracy looked down at us, her tiny face locked in terror. B palmed me out of the way as he took the stairs two at a time. Tracy screamed and ran into her bedroom. B ordered her to stop but she ran in and locked the door. He was pounding on the door by the time I caught up with him. I still held the knife I had been peeling the potatoes with.

'Move away from that door,' I said calmly as I held the knife out in front of me.

B looked up. 'You wouldn't dare.'

I took a step forward. 'Move away from that door or you'll have the biggest backache you'll ever remember.'

He turned to face me and tried to bluff me again holding up his fists as if prepared for confrontation. B looked into my eyes and at that moment knew I couldn't have been more serious.

'Make a move then, you spineless bastard,' I said, gritting

my teeth, holding the knife up to face level. I took another step forward.

B bottled it. He threw in the towel.

He lowered his fists and said something about not wanting to see the kids anyway. He eased his way past me carefully, trying to force a smile and almost ran out of the house. The spineless yellow coward was never seen again for months.

***

At the age of 24, I had struck up a friendship with a man who I will call simply Tom, not his real name. I told him from the start I had two kids and didn't do boyfriends, but there was something different about Tom I liked. He wasn't cocky and never made a pass at me. It seemed that all he was looking for was a friendship. It worked well. The last thing I wanted, after all I'd been through, was another man.

We talked about things we liked, and about our wishes for the future. We were like best mates. I never felt uncomfortable with him, and I found myself spending more and more time with him. He took me on my first real date to the Béarnaise Steak House at the Pier Head. I had never seen a menu before and couldn't make sense of it, but I bluffed my way through and asked him to choose for me. We had prawn cocktail, steak and chips and a lemon sorbet. Adventurous or what?

Tom seemed at his happiest when he took me and the girls out for day trips in his car. The girls loved him and before I knew it we were like one big happy family. Looking back, those days were some of the happiest I can remember. I was rid of B, had my own independence, two beautiful girls, Mum and Dad, my brothers and my neighbours, and now a man who genuinely seemed to like me for what I was. He was like a real dad to my girls, buying things, helping them and taking us out, and they adored him. This was what a father should be like, I thought.

I started to feel like it was all too good to be true. I was waiting for the bubble to burst and began to feel vulnerable again. I was getting too close to Tom and wondered when the abuse would start as it had with B. When was he going to start shouting and smacking me about? I was like a cat on a hot tin roof waiting for it, believing that it was just around the corner.

Incredibly, I even started goading Tom at times, making up little arguments on purpose, waiting for that first fight. I hadn't told Tom anything about my previous marriage other than we were divorced and, like the gentleman that he was, he never asked. But I felt that Tom needed to know and I had to find a way to tell him, a way to warn him of the emotional and psychological scars I was carrying and the mess he was getting himself into. Looking back now on the incident I'm about to describe, I firmly believe I was putting Tom to the test.

He'd called round to see me one day and everything was very pleasant. We had a cup of tea and he made some plans for the weekend to take the girls to Southport. I watched him sitting at the table drinking from the cup. It seemed he hadn't a care in the world. I excused myself and went into the bathroom. I looked around and found a tube of toothpaste. The tube was made out of a thin metal and I unrolled it right out, unfurled the bottom bit and prised it apart, leaving two thin strips of razor-sharp metal. I sliced myself three times across the stomach until the blood ran down to the waistband of my skirt. I then replaced my blouse and casually walked towards the door.

He was sitting in exactly the same position and I stood in the doorway.

'You think you know me, Tom, don't you?'

Tom looked up... Puzzled, he gave a little smile as if to say, 'What are you talking about?'

I pulled my blouse open. 'This is me, Tom,' I said casually.

His face showed sheer terror as he jumped up with a start. He ran over and clutched me hard. But, while I expected a slap across the face, instead he just hugged me with tears in his eyes.

He was shouting, 'Don't you ever do that again. If you want to hurt anyone, then hurt me.'

I pushed him away. 'You don't know me, Tom,' I repeated.

'You idiot,' he was shouting as he looked at the blood dripping on to my skirt.

He came to me again. 'Don't you ever do that again.'

'Or else?' I taunted. 'You'll hit me, is that it?'

Tom was shaking his head.

Surely he'll hit me now, I thought.

But he didn't. He burst into tears.

CHAPTER SIXTEEN

A NEW LEASE OF LIFE

And now 'twas like all instruments,
Now like a lonely flute;
And now it is an angel's song,
That makes the heavens be mute.

There wasn't a bad bone in Tom's body; he would never have hit me in a thousand years. What was going through my head to subject him to that? And then the guilt kicked in: I didn't deserve such a kind man who liked me for just being me.

Nevertheless, I started trying to trust him. It was difficult, in the light of what I'd been through, to trust another man but I took one day at a time. Tom started spending a lot of time at my house and I would spend a few nights each month at his.

We were sitting on the settee one day when he discovered a secret I'd kept hidden since my schooldays. Passing me a newspaper, he pointed at a spot halfway down the page.

'Is that film on BBC1 later on?' he asked.

I stared at the page for a minute or so. 'Yes,' I replied.

He looked across at me. 'You can't read, can you?'

'Of course I can read,' I said defensively. 'What makes you think that?'

'Because that isn't the television page,' he said.

I had left school without a single qualification, barely able to read or write a few words. In the years that followed, I never gave reading or writing a thought. As I grew older, it was harder to pick up the pieces but easier to blag my way through.

I'd managed up to now, managed to shop and feed and clothe the children, write my signature here and there when necessary. I told Tom I could read enough to go into shops and that was enough. Who needed newspapers and books when we had TV? Tom pointed out that I had managed to shop because the tins in the supermarkets had pictures of their contents on the sides, and of course a bag of potatoes was a bag of potatoes. But he also said that, if I couldn't read, I was missing out on a whole lot of wonderful books.

It brought back memories of my earliest days at school. The teacher took me to the cloakroom and showed me a picture of an umbrella while saying, 'That is where your coat goes.' It was picture association: you see a picture, they tell you what it is and you have to remember it. I'd seen the word associated with the picture of the umbrella and therefore could spell umbrella without any problems. At a rough guess, I could probably spell 20 to 25 words and one of them was the word 'umbrella'.

But I was ashamed that Tom had discovered my secret and more than a little annoyed at the questions he was asking me. I expected him to burst out laughing at any minute but of course he never did. Instead, he decided that he was going to do his best to try to teach me to read, and to encourage me to seek help.

He must have had the patience of a saint; he set me a task to learn three words a day. I thought I'd be about 100 by the time I could read properly but each day brought a new joy and understanding of new words and their meaning. Despite not wanting to admit it, I was actually enjoying learning again. At one point, everything in the house had a sticker on it to say what it was: iron, cooker, fridge, cup, pan, table.

If I cleaned up and the stickers fell off, it was like a jigsaw puzzle trying to put them back into place again but I managed and within a few short months could spell everything in the house correctly. It was working and I was surprised how easy it was.

When I first got to grips with long words and sentences, I used to love going into card shops and reading all the cards stacked on the shelves and on stands. I would spend hours in card shops reading card after card, absorbing the words. Cards were an easy read and cards would say nice things about you, even when you were dead. Maybe people should be more like cards, then they would be nice to you all the time.

After about a year of Tom's help with reading, he insisted that I go along to an adult learning centre that he'd heard about in Prescot. I felt uncomfortable at the thought of going back to school again, but as soon as I walked through the door I knew I had made the right decision. I was part of a group of a similar level to me and we all became great friends.

Soon my mind became like a sponge, wanting to absorb everything. I devoured the contents of magazines and papers, and eventually moved on to library books. I had been so very afraid of the library, afraid of all those thousands of books stacked up on the hundreds of shelves, millions and trillions of words printed there for me to fall into and get lost. I was afraid that they would remind me how stupid I still was.

My teacher advised me to learn to channel what I was doing because I was flying off at a tangent. She suggested I stuck to books on a particular subject and I chose the great painters. I always marvelled at how some people could look at a painting and then say, 'That's a Monet,' or 'That's a van Gogh.' How did they do that? I soon learned through reading the art books in the library that it was simply down to the style of the painter. Before I started to read those, I didn't know any painters, except, that is, for Magnolia Joe who was a house painter that lived round the corner. They called him Magnolia Joe because he was always covered in spots of magnolia paint.

I was determined to read all I could about the great painters and there were so many. I saw a film where Peter Sellers played the French painter Toulouse-Lautrec, or, to give him his full name, Henri Marie Raymond de Toulouse-Lautrec-Monfa. I learned all I could about him and then went on to learn about the women he painted. His paintings were different; to me they were exciting, elegant and even a little provocative. He painted images of the modern and sometimes decadent life of those times. He was without a doubt one of the greatest painters of the Post-Impressionist era. And if that last sentence or two sounds a little fancy and goes against the writing style of Crissy Rock, then you are correct because I learned that from a book. Wonderful, isn't it?

I could also sympathise with Toulouse-Lautrec, as he didn't exactly have it too easy in his early life, dogged with health problems, suffering from a then unknown genetic disorder called osteoporosis. He broke both thigh bones in his early teens and consequently his legs stopped growing. Toulouse was only five foot tall as an adult but that did not stop him painting some of the greatest works of art ever. To see what I mean, take a look at paintings like *Vincent van Gogh*, *In Bed* (that's not 'Vincent van Gogh in bed', but two separate paintings), *The Clown Cha-U-Kao at the Moulin Rouge*, *Salon at the Rue des Moulins* and the stylistic departure of something like *Ambassadeurs: Aristide Bruant*. Anyway, I'm showing off now but I hope one day to stand in front of a Toulouse-Lautrec painting or even visit his birthplace in the Pyrenees, because I feel he played such an important role in my life in discovering both the written word and the power of education.

I also studied Leonardo da Vinci, Claude Monet, Vincent van Gogh and Pablo Picasso. The more I learned, the more I wanted to find out. I once visited Amsterdam and stood in front of a Vincent van Gogh painting. I was completely entranced by it, and I started to cry as I moved up close and saw the strokes where his brush had been. I discovered that van Gogh had been a friend of Toulouse-Lautrec, and, like him, had died only in his mid-thirties.

You never ever stop learning, and that is the beauty of education. You don't need a cap and gown, and it's great to see someone's face when you can hold a conversation about things they think you don't know anything about, particularly if they have prejudged you because of a dialect or accent. For me, learning to read was a particular revelation. It seemed as if, overnight, my life had changed beyond all recognition.

It's fair to say that on the whole the next 10 years of my life were good ones, although I still had periods where the emotional baggage I carried came to the surface and affected me badly. I suffered a series of nervous breakdowns, but I always fought through them.

Tom and I decided to get married in 1989. I had been deprived of a white wedding the first time around and quite naturally assumed we would do the church bit with Dad walking me down the aisle. Tom was dead against it and said he would only get married if we told no one and disappeared to a quiet registry office. I still harboured feelings of insecurity and felt a wedding ring would make Tom my girls' official dad, and make my life complete. I reluctantly agreed and dropped the girls off at Mum's one weekend under the pretence that we were off to Wales for a weekend.

The wedding was very low-key with Tom's brother and his girlfriend as the witnesses. Afterwards, we went to the local pub. When I remarked to Tom that I'd had two weddings but never had a wedding cake, he rushed out of the pub to a baker's along the street. He came back with a strawberry tart and said at least I had some wedding cake now. He meant it as a nice gesture, but I didn't really see it that way.

Back at Mum and Dad's, they were devastated at what I had done. Mum cried and cried saying that I'd been married twice and she hadn't been to either of the weddings. Dad ranted on at what a selfish cow I was, depriving him of walking his only daughter down the aisle.

They were right, and if I could turn the clock back I would. I should have been more forceful with Tom and at least demanded a small wedding, even if it had been just parents and immediate family.

It was four years into our marriage when I first noticed that Tom's drinking levels had begun to increase. Perhaps I'd never noticed, and maybe Tom had managed to drink in secret for longer than I thought, but, around the time I was preparing to take my first real steps on the stage, I began to notice worrying signs.

Tom had always liked a drink. His job as a shopfitter for his brother's firm took him all over the country and, obviously, when he worked away I could never gauge the amount of alcohol he was consuming. If he was working in the North of England, he would be home just about every night, and if he worked locally he would call in at the pub every night on the way home from work.

'Just for a couple,' he would say. 'It's a tradition, washes the dust from the throat.'

I couldn't really argue. Tom worked in a dusty environment and for the first few years it was 'just a couple'. Then an hour or two in the pub gradually turned into three and four. I made a few comments about him not seeing me and the children enough, and for a few months he went back to the 'just a couple' habit. What was I worrying about? I asked myself; Tom was only a social drinker and he'd just proved it. Yet somehow, and I couldn't put my finger on it, something gnawed away inside me that the picture Tom was painting wasn't quite true.

***

I have always been a bit of a clown; sometimes I used it as a mask to hide my pain but, yes, I'm always there with a quick comment or a witty remark. Whatever shit life throws at me, without even thinking about it I manage to find the slightest chink of humour in most situations. I think a lot of people in Liverpool are like that; I've met hundreds of comics in the city that have never set foot on a stage and never will but they are the funniest people you will ever come across. The make-up of the people of Liverpool is unique, the sort I've not encountered anywhere else. They are resilient and always try to look on the bright side of life.

The city has the same problems as any other inner city in the UK, but the people of Liverpool are slighty different and on the whole welcome strangers with open arms. History shows us that Liverpool is made up from a huge influx of Irish immigrants who crossed the Irish Sea (and further afield) to escape the poverty and persecution by the British government during the potato famine of 1845–51.

The immigrants of Ireland were forced to leave their homeland and then faced the many problems all immigrants faced: trying to settle and make a living in towns and cities where no one wanted them. They were well and truly at rock bottom. This is just my theory and I may be wrong, but I believe they learned to survive by laughing and talking about the predicament they were in. As they recovered and prospered, they laughed all the more, and eventually exorcised their demons by pushing away any resentment and bitterness. They moved on through the power of laughter, and it is this spirit which Liverpool still retains, thanks in no small part to the Irish immigrants from the mid-19th century.

I am exactly the same. Cracking a joke or laughing about something helps me to move on, helps me to think that perhaps things are getting a little better. When I go back to Liverpool and sit with my brothers and laugh about the old days, it is generally the bad old days we invariably end up talking about.

In the spring of 1986, we were all sitting in a pub watching the Grand National on TV. Grand National day is always a special day in Liverpool – the race is held at the city's Aintree racecourse – and everything stops 20 minutes before the race starts. Even the kick-off times for Liverpool and Everton fixtures are altered so that no one misses that race. I had picked about four or five horses and, true to form, I joked about every one of them as they fell or if they were still running when the next race started. I couldn't pick my nose, let alone a reliable horse, but I didn't care because people were laughing. One of my friends picked up a beer mat and threw it across the table.

'Look at this, Crissy,' she said. 'The brewery is sponsoring a comedian of the year competition. Why don't you enter?'

'Behave yourself,' I said. 'I'm not a comic.'

But as my other friends were studying the beer mats, they encouraged me all the more to enter. Eventually, my cousin Janet bet me a pound that I wouldn't enter. I shook her hand and took her up on the challenge.

In the cold light of day the next morning, I shit myself. I wanted to pull out but knew I would face some hostile questioning from my friends and, in particular, Janet. I made up my mind that I would rather give it a go even if I died on stage than walk into the pub admitting I'd bottled it.

The rules of the competition were simple: you had three minutes to impress the judges. Three minutes was an awfully long time. What would I talk about? Inspiration came from the disaster of my first marriage. I decided to devise a three-minute monologue in which I would play the downtrodden wife.

The audition was on the top floor of a pub, The Old Swan, in the Dovecote area of the city. Three people in suits from the brewery were there to judge my performance, but their faces showed no emotion, let alone a hint of a smile or a laugh. I started off by telling them they were looking at a woman with only two weeks to live. I told them my husband had buggered off for a fortnight. At this, one of the judges cracked a smile and I was off, living off my wits and ad libbing as usual.

'My husband asked me the other day why I never tell him when I orgasm... Because you're never there, I said.'

All three judges were smiling now.

'I whispered the three special words to him last night when we were in bed... is it in?'

More smiles, one was even laughing out loud.

'I shouldn't skit him really, he's good in bed... till I get in.'

In the end, they told me my time was up and, although I had overrun, the fact that they were still listening to me was a good sign... I thought!

Anyway, who was I kidding? I'd enjoyed the experience but I wasn't a comedienne. There were hundreds, maybe thousands in for the competition. I had no chance.

Two weeks later, I got a letter to say that I was through to the next round and my heat would be at the Horseshoe pub in Whiston. Bloody hell!

I worked hard on perfecting my routine, ironing out the inconsistencies in my story so that it flowed a little easier, and so that each joke picked up from where the previous one left off.

I won that heat. I was then informed that the next round was at the Farmer's Arms in Huyton.

Oh my God, that's where I live. What if someone I know sees me?

I plucked up the courage to go through with it thanks to the support of my friends who wouldn't hear of me quitting now. I dreaded walking on to the stage at Huyton but thankfully most of the audience was in the dark so I didn't see anyone I recognised.

Eventually, I was runner-up in the north-west region. I told them that was to be expected because I'd never won anything in my life. 'I'm even my husband's second wife,' I joked, as they presented me with a cheque for £100.

CHAPTER SEVENTEEN

TRUE BLUE

Oh! dream of joy! is this indeed
The lighthouse top I see?
Is this the hill? is this the kirk?
Is this mine own country?

My success didn't bring any job offers immediately. I just carried on with living my normal life. People who had seen me perform began asking me to do charity nights for free, and of course I was only too happy to oblige. I did as many charity events as I could – they were real hands-on experiences, and a good foundation to developing an act.

My first real paid gig was at the Montrose Club just off Breck Road in Everton, for which I was paid £40. I was frozen to the spot with terror when my name was announced there – this was no charity event but the real thing – but the compère had spotted similar signs of nerves in a thousand other performers, and so more or less pushed me to the centre of the stage. My hands were flapping about so much I could hardly hold the mike. Nevertheless, a minute or two into my set, I came into my own. Not only was I getting more comfortable with each performance but I was actually beginning to enjoy being up there.

At another charity event, Iggy Navarro was in the audience. Iggy had played Shake Hands in the *Boys from the Black Stuff* on TV. Iggy said I had talent and the potential to turn professional. He fine-tuned my act, taught me about the timing and advised me how to make punchlines more powerful. His wife ran a club in Shield Road in the city and he put me to work on the stage after hours. He'd put music on to distract me; it helped me concentrate. He told me never to be afraid; when I complained that there was no audience, he'd tell me that some nights I wouldn't have an audience, either because Liverpool would be playing at home or it would be pissing down with rain.

Iggy taught me everything and as my act got better a few paid gigs came in. Nothing spectacular but I was happy getting £50 a night, two or three times each month. The only thing I wasn't happy about was having to pay a driver to take me to and from gigs. I swear some nights the driver was earning more than me and of course the petrol was on top. With the agency fee, I was lucky to clear £20 from a £50 fee and then of course tax was always deducted. There had to be a better way to keep a little more of my fee.

I met an agent called Lyn Staunton soon after. She described me as a rough diamond, which is where the name Rock came from. Lyn and her husband Tom were instrumental in starting the process of polishing the Rock into something resembling a diamond, albeit a bit of an industrial one. When I spoke to Lyn just recently, she predicted this book would become a best-seller, and asked if I'd give her company Power Productions a plug. OK, there you are, Lyn, told you I'd put it in. Would I lie to you? Power Productions, there you go again, two for the price of one. LOL…

I decided to learn to drive and managed to pay for some lessons. I had 11 lessons but could not cope with the gearstick. After five lessons, my driving instructor could take no more of my kangaroo starts and suggested we switch to an automatic. Trying to change gear was like trying to rub my belly and tap my head at the same time. I just couldn't do it.

With the money from the gigs, I paid for the lessons. I was worried about the fact that, even though I could just about read now, there were a lot of words I couldn't get my head round and I wondered if I would be good enough to read the Highway Code. Jesus, it felt like trying to memorise *War and Peace.*

Nevertheless, in the early 1990s, I put in for my test. I got a phone call some weeks later. The lady from the driving school told me there were two dates available: 1 April and, a few days later, a space on Friday, 13 April. That's me… little Miss Lucky! I begged her for another date but she claimed there was nothing for weeks. It was plainly obvious nobody wanted those dates so I plumped for 1 April. I turned up on the morning of April Fools' Day a bundle of nerves. The examiner turned to face me as I climbed into the car; I smiled, wound down the window, stuck my head out and vomited on to the roadside. He was horrified and asked me if I wanted to postpone my test.

'No thanks,' I said, 'my head will start spinning in a minute and I'll be OK after that.' The joke was lost on him.

'Don't worry, love,' he said. 'Not many people pass their driving test first time.'

Good start, I thought. That's right, build up my confidence, why don't you?

I was determined to prove him wrong and concentrated harder than I had ever concentrated on anything before. He pointed to a car down the street and asked me to read the number plate.

'That's not my car,' I said. Not a great start. Nevertheless, I felt the driving part of the test went well and before long we were on to the Highway Code.

He showed me a sign with a black shape in the middle. I recognised the sign and began to relax.

'A humpty back bridge,' I said confidently.

He smiled. 'Well, actually it's a humpback bridge but I'll give you it.'

He looked at me seriously. 'You're driving on a motorway with a roof rack on and your case falls off on to the motorway. What would you do?'

It was a trick question and I'd seen right through it.

I smiled. 'I wouldn't be on the motorway 'cause I haven't passed me test.'

He repeated the question seriously. 'You're driving on a motorway with a roof rack on and your case falls off on to the motorway. What would you do?'

'Does that mean I've passed?' I said.

'Errrr, not yet, just answer the question please.' He raised his voice a little. 'Pretend you have passed your test and your suitcase has fallen into the middle of the motorway. What would you do?'

I thought about it for a second. 'Nothing.'

'Nothing?' he replied. 'And why not?'

'Because I haven't got a roof rack.'

'Pretend you've got a bloody roof rack.'

Oh dear, he was losing his temper.

'I haven't got a suitcase either.'

'Pretend!' he shouted. 'Pretend you've passed your bloody test and you've got a bloody suitcase and a bloody roof rack. Now, what would you do?'

'I'd pull on to the hard shoulder and try to retrieve the suitcase if it wasn't too dangerous and if I couldn't I'd report it to the police.'

He looked at me and smiled and I noticed him drawing a little tick on his sheet of paper.

'Correct,' he said. 'And why would you do that?'

'Because I haven't got a suitcase, which would mean I'd borrowed it off me dad and he'd murder me if I'd lost it.'

The examiner shook his head and folded his piece of paper and put it into a small briefcase. He shook his head again and then smiled.

I passed. At the age of 33, I had my first qualification. I bought a BM (a battered Marina). It cost £50, had six months' MOT and, more importantly, an automatic gearbox. I was up and running, and for the first time in my life had a little independence.

* * *

Unfortunately, things on the home front had taken a slight turn for the worse. Tom had continued his after-work evening ritual of a couple of hours in the pub but had also started bringing back cans of beer to drink at home. Now I was really beginning to get worried. I expressed my concerns several times and he said that, as long as it didn't affect his ability to get up and do a day's work, it was none of my business. I comforted myself by believing him.

Several weeks later, though, Tom came home and told me he'd been laid off. I would only find out months later that he'd been sacked because of his drinking. His brother had given him chance after chance but he'd been let down too often. My darling husband at that time had a major drink problem and I didn't know it. I felt sorry for Tom as he became depressed. All the while, he kept up the pretence that he'd been let go because there was no work. In the time that followed, if he wasn't out and about looking for work, he spent most of his time at home.

At least my comedy work paid the bills and went towards a few luxuries too. Iggy was continuing to push me and help me learn the business. I have lived and died working as a comic, because, if you've never died on stage, you've never lived as a comic. It's tough, one of the hardest jobs in the world, but when I'm on stage it makes me feel at home because I turn into Crissy Rock. It's all one big act when I'm up there; what you see is not what you get. Crissy Rock is confident, cocky, has a certain swagger and a couldn't-care-less attitude to life. The real me is far different. I wish I could be like Crissy Rock offstage.

Some of the clubs I performed at was like working in a morgue; sometimes I went down like the *Titanic* but always learned to fight another day. Some you win and some you lose. I remember going to a working men's club in Wigan once. Talk about a bad gig! In Wigan, when people die, they put them in an audience when a comic's on stage. My first few gags didn't even raise a smile; they just sat there as if on autopilot lifting their drinks to their mouths every few minutes. When I came off, the concert secretary came into my dressing room. I decided that attack was the best form of defence.

'Look, mate, I'm sorry,' I said. 'I did my best and, if you don't want to pay me, I'll understand.'

The poor bloke looked at me with the strangest look on his face. 'Are you kidding, love?' he replied. 'They loved you. That was the best reception anyone has had for a long time. If they didn't like you, they would have thrown you out the side door. That's what happened with one comic last week.'

I got my money and another booking two weeks later.

An audience is like a dog, and a dog can smell fear, and if they sense fear you have lost it. You have to be strong and, even if you die on your arse, you can't take it personally. It's just a job at the end of the day and everyone has off days. My mum even came to see me once or twice too. By this time she was in a wheelchair. Her kidneys were failing and her heart was weak. She was not in good health but I was so proud she made the effort to come and see me. She sat in the audience in her wheelchair as quiet as a mouse with a permanent little smile on her face.

I'd wait for the first heckler. I'd point at Mum. 'That's my mum over there. You'd better be careful because I'll knock you out and she'll run you over.'

Mum didn't quite know where to put herself, but I think she enjoyed the attention in her own sort of way.

Mum couldn't get out much by now, and relied on Dad and me to take her places. I took Mum to see the film *Shirley Valentine*. There's a part in that film where Shirley, played by Pauline Collins, says, 'If we're given all this life, why are we not allowed to use it?' With Mum in a wheelchair from the age of only 42, that's the part of the film that still makes me cry. Poor Mum never had the chance to enjoy her life, particularly in the last 10 years. And yet she never complained once.

Thankfully, Mum was not there the night I performed in

a club not far from Birmingham, just off the M5. Jesus, it was rough. The patrons had gold sovereigns on every finger of every hand and noses that spread all over their faces... and that was just the women! Before I even opened my mouth, a bloke from the audience shouted, 'Fuck off back to Liverpool.'

'Sorry,' I retorted, 'I don't do requests.'

I was due to be on for 45 minutes, but every few minutes the heckler was up on his feet shouting again. He didn't have much in the way of vocabulary – mostly he was just shouting 'fuck off'. It was going to be a long night, but I plodded on regardless. Fifteen minutes to go and he still hadn't relented, so I decided to take him on. By now, he wasn't even bothering to stand up, merely sitting at a table with his drinking pals shouting things like 'Fuck off' and 'You're shit'.

I took a step forward and fronted him up. 'Of all the millions of sperm that dies, I can't believe that yours fucking got through.'

His jaw hit the floor. It was the first time I had ever sworn on stage and a momentary hush fell over the audience as people began to sit up and take notice. It didn't stop him though.

'Fuck off.'

Why wasn't this man getting thrown out of the club? I thought. I looked around for some movement, a sign that a doorman or a member of the committee was on his way. Nothing.

'Fuck off.'

I looked over at him again. I struggled hard to maintain my composure.

'Look,' I said, 'if you're going to heckle me, can you

heckle me with at least one or two more words, you thick get. Show a little intelligence. You've obviously never heard of a dictionary.'

'Fuck off, you slag.'

'Oh, be still, my beating heart,' I mocked, patting my chest. 'Are you confusing me for your mother?'

He rose to his feet. 'If you were a fucking man, I'd punch you.'

'If I was a man, short arse, you'd be in a fucking coma right now.'

By this time, his mates and the rest of the audience were laughing at him. All of a sudden, he didn't look so self-assured.

It still didn't stop him.

'Fuck off,' he repeated.

He sat down.

I sighed. 'Those words again. If you were one of the seven dwarfs in a pantomime, mate, I bet you'd play fucking Dopey.'

'Fuck off.'

'What's the matter? Are you out tonight because the MENSA meeting has been cancelled?'

And the battle continued, and if the truth be told I was beginning to enjoy it. I felt I had the upper hand.

'If your dick was as big as your mouth, you might have a fucking girl with you.'

The final insult he threw at me was to ask what a Scouse dick tasted like.

'I don't know,' I said. 'Ask your sister.'

A little quieter this time: 'Fuck off.'

'Look, mate, if you're trying to get in my knickers, forget it, because there's only room for one fucking arsehole in there.'

Almost a whisper now: 'Fuck off.'

'Ahhh…' I said, 'now I know what contraception you use. Your fucking personality.'

Silence.

I'd won.

Dickhead was hoping for the ground to open up so he could crawl into the hole. He visibly shrank into his seat and even in the dim light I could see the embarrassment on his face shining like a beacon.

I must confess that last 15 minutes went a lot quicker than the first half an hour. When my time was up, I looked over to him again. 'OK, mate, I'm fucking off now, not because you want me to fuck off but because I want to fuck off. You, my friend, can fuck right off yourself.'

He never said a word.

As I walked off the stage, people rose to their feet and gave me a standing ovation. I looked back to his table; even his mates were on their feet applauding me as Dopey sat rooted firmly to his chair.

I may have won the battle but as far as I was concerned I'd lost the war. I'd lowered myself to his level of the gutter. My fee was £45; I kissed it goodbye.

There was a knock on the door and the chairman of the club came into the dressing room. I began to apologise. The man was shaking his head as he handed me an envelope with £50 in it.

'Keep the change,' he said, waving his hand. 'Can you come back next week?' he continued. 'You were fantastic.'

I shook my head in amazement.

'Only next week can you be blue from the beginning? I'll double your money.'

'Eh?'

'Swear and curse from the beginning, love. Blue comedians get double the rate of pay at this club.'

TRUE BLUE

I was absolutely flabbergasted. But there you have it: the story of why and when I turned into a blue comedienne.

CHAPTER EIGHTEEN

ANOTHER GOODBYE

If she may know which way to go;
For she guides him smooth or grim.
See, brother, see! how graciously
She looketh down on him.'

Nothing prepares you for losing your mother because you automatically think she will go on forever, no matter how poor her health is. Mums don't die, mums shouldn't die. Mine was always there to comfort me when I was down or upset, and, when she died in July 1991, I couldn't come to terms with the fact that I'd never again see her smiling face, touch her soft skin or smell the beautiful smell she had. Oh, how I wish I could have bottled that smell.

My brothers took it badly too. Mum died just four days after our youngest brother Jason had his 16th birthday party. As for Dad, he was devastated and in shock for weeks, like a lost soul.

It's strange how people say the funniest things in grief. A few days after she died, Dad got us all together and we sat in the kitchen. He made us strong, sweet cups of tea and it was clear he was about to deliver a comforting speech to his beloved children, something rallying, something for us to take comfort from, so that we could move on with our lives.

Dad sat down and nursed his cup of tea with both hands as we awaited his soothing words.

'Mum's gone and nothing I can say will bring her back.' He took a sip of tea and continued. 'I know it's hard for you…' He paused and looked up. 'But it's even harder for me… I'll miss her more because I knew her longer.'

We laughed through our tears, and Dad wondered what the hell we were all laughing at. He didn't realise what he'd said was so soft!

It was amazing how the family and friends rallied round, not just for a few days but for months and years afterwards. Auntie Jean, Dad's sister, was always there, as was Linda, who was mum to my brother David's girlfriend. Linda was always very close to our mum and spent a lot of time looking after Dad after Mum died. She'd bring him odd meals and tidy up and clean for him. She was divorced and they became very close. After a few months, they started going out together. Dad had every right to move on and find someone else. No one could accuse him of any wrongdoing and when Mum was alive he worshipped the ground she walked on, and loved her with all his heart.

I think it's fair to say that some of my brothers thought he could have waited a little longer before moving another woman into Mum's space. Brian in particular wasn't too happy with the new domestic arrangements. But nothing was mentioned until the death of Dad's dog, Cindy. It affected Dad badly, he was in a terrible state, and so I rang my brothers and we all went round to offer some support. Jesus, the house was like a morgue. Linda was sitting on the settee with her arm round him and it was clear he had been crying. He sat and stared into space with a wet handkerchief in his hands. We waited with bated breath for his first words.

He wiped his eyes. 'That's it. I will never get another dog.' He was heartbroken.

'Why not, Dad?' I asked.

'Because nothing could ever replace Cindy.'

Brian could not contain himself and jumped to his feet. The feelings he'd bottled up for so long surfaced. 'Nothing could replace Cindy!' he shouted. 'Nothing could replace Cindy,' he repeated. 'Oh no, nothing could replace Cindy.' He pointed to Linda. 'But you replaced me bloody mum quick enough though, didn't you?'

All hell broke loose with more tears and shouting and, if I remember right, Brian stormed out of the house. Linda had done nothing but be kind to my dad, keeping him company after Mum died, and I guess they just fell in love.

Thankfully, the row didn't fester – I suppose Brian had got what he needed to say off his chest – and before long the incident was all forgotten. Ten years later, my dad and Linda went on to marry, and I really couldn't have wished for anyone better for Dad. They had a lovely wedding day, and I felt so pleased for Dad and how happy he was. My brothers and I sat together. We cried tears of joy and, of course, a few tears of sadness too – as we hadn't forgotten our mum and couldn't help but feel that she'd been taken from all of us far too young.

I thank you, Mum, for all the joy and laughter you brought into all our lives. You are kept in my heart and I still ask you for advice when I am up there on stage. You float above me like the angel that you were. I know you are always close by and while I have you in my heart you will never leave me.

CHAPTER NINETEEN

MY BIG BREAK

O happy living things! no tongue
Their beauty might declare:
A spring of love gushed from my heart,
And I blessed them unaware:
Sure my kind saint took pity on me,
And I blessed them unaware

My big national break on television had occurred in the late eighties. I'd applied to go on TV's *Opportunity Knocks* hosted by one of my all-time favourite comedians, Bob Monkhouse. If I remember rightly, it was my friends and family who convinced me to apply, and when I was invited for an audition in London I made the excuse that I couldn't afford the train ticket to London. (A little convenient white lie.)

True to form, that didn't stop them. They got together and because the soap powder manufacturer Flash were running an Inter-City rail promotion they all started to buy boxes of Flash for the cardboard coupons on the back of the box. Thirty-five coupons equalled a return fare to London and the wonderful, wonderful people tricked me into going to the pub one night where they presented me with my ticket. How could I refuse to go to London now? It was the sort of gesture that was typical of Liverpool's community spirit. I swear that, with the number of coupons collected, half the pub could have travelled to bloody London.

I made it through the audition, and on to the show itself. Bob Monkhouse took a real shine to me because I was a comic. He complimented me on my timing which he said was one of the best he'd ever seen. Wow! I did well in my heat, and was only beaten by a set of 'Irish dancers'... who hailed from Scotland!

My appearance on the show meant that, afterwards, I was getting more live bookings than ever. At my peak, I was earning £2,000–3,000 most months, which was big money then. Tom didn't need to find a job any more, as I had now turned professional and a top agency had taken me on.

Roger Davis became my agent. He had come to see me in a working men's club and approached me after the show. I took a chance with him taking me on as a client – it was gut instinct – and, with his help, my reputation and success went from strength to strength. Roger helped me to get the right contacts that gave me work all over the country.

There was a downside to this success. I didn't realise it at the time, but I was working too much, afraid that every job could be my last, and was overlooking the problems at home. Night after night in all weathers, I was driving up and down the M62, M58 and M6, taking every job I was offered.

Thankfully, Auntie Jean, my dad's oldest sister, was accompanying me to most of the gigs. She had lost her son, our cousin Stephen, just before his 21st birthday, when he was killed in a car crash – tragically while he was travelling to my brother Ian's wedding. Stephen was buried on Friday, 13 October 1989 and Ian was married the following day.

Auntie Jean had become like a mother to me; her children were her life and, after Stephen's death, I swear half of her died. Stephen's own son – also called Stephen and who she adored – kept her going through her grief. In turn, Auntie Jean would be my soulmate after Mum's death, and I hope I helped her through dark days after her son's death. Coming with me to all four corners of England gave Auntie Jean a new interest in life and we talked for hours during those long journeys about life in general, the good old days, and how cruel the hand of fate could be sometimes. Auntie Jean was a real comfort to me. My number-one fan, she came to almost every show, and didn't even seem to mind the language I was using on stage. (At least, she never mentioned anything.)

Even if she didn't accompany me to a show, she would phone constantly and check that I drove home safely. Stephen's car accident had clearly left a huge mental scar that she just couldn't get over. Every time someone she cared about climbed into a car, she thought the worst. Yet she was perfectly happy getting into a car and driving for miles.

The hardest part for me was finding the places I had to go to, but Auntie Jean was a good navigator. Some clubs were in the back of beyond. I remember once I performed at Sizewell B power station down in Suffolk, and it took nearly all day to get there. It didn't look that far on the map and Auntie Jean thought it was just down the road. Sizewell B power station... And you think show business is all glamour?

Performing in the summer time was tough, especially in the school holidays, because you could never plan a holiday or even a weekend away. I was working every Friday, every Saturday and occasionally a Sunday. That's when your family suffers, I think, but I was paranoid that, if I turned down the gigs, they would simply start looking for someone else. I was also enjoying the benefits of money in my pocket for once and lavished new clothes and gifts on the girls. As a working mother, I provided the money for all the luxuries my girls and Tom enjoyed, but it never replaces that precious family time that is lost forever. I would have liked to have spent more time shopping with the girls or an occasional Saturday night out with Tom at a restaurant, but, every time something was planned, a phone call from the agency would ruin it.

As I've said, I've made mistakes along the way and I confess that I was out of the house too much trying to build a name for myself. I craved financial security for my girls and this was the only way I could see it happening. Some would say I craved fame; that was simply not true. Throughout my life, I'd lived with poverty and suddenly there was a financial light at the end of the tunnel and I was determined to grab it with both hands. I loved being able to provide for my girls, things I'd never had, spoiling them. I love both my girls very much and, although I would not have won Mother of the Year, I hope that I have been a mother they can be proud of and love just the same. And I hope, by reading this book, Tracy and Hayley may understand a little more of what it was I was trying to achieve and why.

* * *

In mid-1993, I took a phone call from the secretary of Ricky Tomlinson's agency, ART Casting in Liverpool's Camden Street. Ricky had established quite a successful business starting with a single office that he slept in to save on expenses as he was living in Wales at the time. Though I hadn't met Ricky at this point, I had heard of his agency. I didn't know it at the time but Ricky had seen me perform many times and had made a point of getting in touch with my agency. Things were going well. I wasn't looking for anything grand in life, I was just happy I had a job, especially one I loved doing, and one that provided a home and other nice things for my family.

Ricky's secretary explained that they were calling club acts to audition for some kind of film. The auditions were to be held at the Dockers' Club in Liverpool. I explained to the lady that it didn't really appeal to me as I certainly wasn't an actress and deep down I knew people like me were only used as extras. I had enough to do without being stuck in the middle of a film set all hours of the day and night. The lady explained that Ricky had asked for me personally. Yeah, yeah, pull the other one, I thought; I bet she says that to everyone she calls.

Then, when fear and insecurity kicked in again, I had a change of heart. I reasoned that this was an opportunity for some more income if, perchance, the comedy work dried up. I didn't know how much an extra made in a film, but I figured that if I turned them down this time they would never call again and I would never know.

When I arrived at the Dockers' Club, it was full of different people of all shapes and sizes, some of whom I recognised from the club scene. They were all discussing their pictures and portfolios of their careers to date. 'This is me in *Casualty*,' they would be saying, or 'This is me in *The Bill*.'

I didn't even have a passport photo with me.

When it was my turn to go upstairs and audition, I was shown into a small office. There was a man already in there. He had a denim shirt on and was sitting very quietly. He looked a little nervous. I assumed that he was there for the audition too and said, 'Hiya, have you come for the audition too?'

He looked up and was just about to speak but, true to form, my mouth was a little bigger and a little quicker. 'I bet you any money that the director will come in with a blue rinse and say, "Hello, ducky."' I mimicked a gay swagger.

'I hope there's no casting couch,' I added, ''cause I'm crap in bed.'

Before he could say a word, the lady that had showed me in came back. 'Crissy, isn't it?'

I nodded.

'This is Ken Loach. He's the director of the film.'

Fuck!

I wanted the ground to open up and swallow me. I nearly died of shame.

Ken Loach was great; he just smiled and asked me what I had done in the past. Nothing, I said. We talked for 10 minutes and he asked if I'd be interested in going down to London for a screen test. I asked him what a screen test was and made a point of telling him I'd never acted in my life. Talk about putting yourself down. However, Ken reassured me that everything would be fine and repeated his offer of a screen test in London one more time. I convinced myself he was just being nice and the secretary of Ricky's agency was probably already drawing up the 'Don't call us, we'll call you' letter.

I was wrong. They even sent me expenses.

Before the journey to London, Ricky Tomlinson met us all at Liverpool Lime Street train station. There were seven of us and he said that we should just be ourselves. It was the first time I'd had a good chat with Ricky and I warmed to him immediately. Nowadays, I count Ricky as one of my best friends; quite simply one of the kindest, most genuine individuals on the planet who will never ever forget where he has come from, unlike some other so-called showbusiness personalities who are all too quick to forget their roots. He put us all on the train and waved us off, wishing us the best of luck. It was Ricky who opened the acting door for me and I will never forget him.

The screen tests for what became *Ladybird Ladybird* were held in Acton in west London. The building looked more like a school and Ken Loach was there overseeing proceedings. When it came to my slot, he talked me through a few of my lines, painted a picture of what he was looking for and told me to improvise the rest. I looked at him rather sheepishly and asked him what improvise meant. It was not a word I had ever heard of, nor could I spell it and again I cursed my lack of education. Ken just smiled and took me through it, explaining in layman's terms exactly what improvisation meant. I had no chance, I thought to myself, as we took the train back home to Liverpool Lime Street. Ken Loach must have been thinking what sort of dimwit Ricky had sent him. And, anyway, people like me don't end up in films, do they?

So I sat on the train and pushed the whole experience to the back of my mind. I closed my eyes and thought about our very first family holiday abroad to Greece. I had saved up for nearly two years. I dreamed of the golden sands and the clear blue sea and the beautiful, hot, sunny days that seemed to have passed Liverpool by of late. I dreamed of nights in Greek tavernas and evening strolls along the water's edge and being a family again. Mostly, I just craved being together, spending quality time with Hayley, Tracy and Tom. I'd never had a holiday like this and I wanted it so much that I started packing our cases a full two weeks before we were due to leave. I'd bought the girls new swimsuits and clothes and leather sandals. Each and every item, some of which still had the price tags on them, was packed ever so carefully into individual cases.

Five days before we were due to leave for the airport, Tom took a phone call. 'It's for you, Crissy, someone called Sally Hibbin.'

I took the phone and shrugged my shoulders. I couldn't remember anyone called Sally Hibbin.

'Hi, Crissy,' she said, 'Sally Hibbin here. I have Ken Loach with me and he wants to speak to you.'

Sally Hibbin was, in fact, the producer of Ken's film. My stomach started to churn. This could only mean one thing: Ken was offering me a part as an extra in his film.

Ken came on the line. 'Hi, Crissy, how are you?'

'Fine, Mr Loach, how are you?'

'Good, good. Listen, Crissy, I've something important to tell you.'

I was thinking, 'Bollocks being an extra, I'm off to Greece with my family. I don't care if they offer me £100 a day. I'm still not doing it.'

'We've given this a lot of thought,' said Ken, 'and we'd like you to play a part in the film *Ladybird Ladybird*.'

'I'm sorry, Mr Loach, I can't. I'm off on holiday with my family. I'm going to Greece at the weekend.'

'Crissy, we'd like you to be the leading actress.'

'The what?'

'The lead role.'

This has to be the biggest wind-up of all time, I thought. Either that or they've made a mistake and rung the wrong person.

'It came down to you and one other girl but we've decided it's you we want,' said Ken.

'You've made a mistake, Mr Loach. I'm not an actress,

give it to the other girl. She's a real actress, I'm just a two-bob comic.'

'Crissy… we want you.'

Tom stood in the passageway. He looked at me and, judging by my reaction, must have thought my entire family had been wiped out in a nuclear explosion. I couldn't speak. Ken sensed exactly what I must have been thinking.

'Take your time, Crissy.'

'I want to go to Greece, Mr Loach.'

'Crissy, give me a call in a day or two. Filming starts next week.'

'I wanna go to Greece.'

I was in tears by the time I hung up. Poor Tom, he didn't have a clue why I was crying so much.

'What is it?' Tom asked.

I blurted out the details between the tears.

Tom's jaw dropped. 'Fucking hell.'

Tom and I sat down at the table and talked between numerous cups of tea. I so wanted to go to Greece. The holiday was my way of thanking my family for putting up with the ridiculously stupid hours I had been working. It was an apology, a gesture to say I can be there with you and that being able to spend such a fabulous holiday all together makes the sacrifices during the rest of the year all worthwhile. I was adamant that I wasn't going to London.

Tom was telling me not to be so stupid; we could have a family holiday any time. This was the opportunity of a lifetime, he said. But I was also full of doubts and was worried about making a fool of myself. I had never acted, I told him. He replied by saying my comedy routine was one big act and that I would cope just fine. Credit to Tom. I don't know how he did it but he managed to talk me round. Even the girls seemed to understand why I wouldn't be going on holiday with them, and there was more than a little fascination and curiosity that Mum might even be appearing on the telly!

I took Tom and the girls to Liverpool Airport and waved them off with a brave face. As soon as they disappeared into Departures for the journey to Greece, I burst out crying.

I also cried on the train all the way to London, cursing Ricky Tomlinson and his secretary for agreeing to the audition in the first place.

I can't really describe my emotional state as I stepped on to the station platform in London. I was in shock, frightened about the thought of making a fool of myself, and, of course, more than a little apprehensive about learning my lines. In the five days since I'd committed to the film, I'd read everything I could get hold of in an attempt to improve and practise my reading ability. I was confident that I could read the part of Maggie Conlan, but remembering the lines was a different matter. And, yes, I admit I was more than a little excited but I was sad too, sad that I wasn't sitting on a beach with my girls on their first holiday abroad. I managed to work my way round London's tube network and found the apartment in Acton that had been rented for me for the next two months.

I unpacked my things, had a wander down Acton High Street and picked up a sandwich and some cans of coke. I returned to the flat and watched a little TV before eventually falling asleep around midnight. Next day, I arrived at a youth centre in Ealing that would be our base for the duration of the filming.

When I got there, I hadn't a clue what the film was even about. Ken met me before we started work and had a long chat with me. Even then I asked him if he was sure I hadn't been cast by mistake. He just laughed. Ken was a father figure to me with endless patience. He would sit and describe the sort of woman the lead was and what she was going through and ask me to imagine what it must be like for her. Maggie Conlan was a victim of domestic violence and, although Ken didn't realise it at the time, I didn't have to try very hard to get into her head.

It became like a jigsaw puzzle for me; because I had never acted before, I never knew what to expect. I was given lines more as a guide and Ken encouraged me to improvise and just go with the flow, and say whatever came into my head. It was a plan that worked well. Ken knew exactly what he was doing and, of course, I was a lot happier knowing that I could deviate a little from the script I was studying. In some scenes, I was given no lines at all, which was just fine by me.

We were filming a bit in a pub one day when Ken came to fetch me. We walked outside and down to a street corner. Ken psyched me up for a few minutes and told me to think about the children I was playing mother to, and what I would do if anything happened to them. That was easy too because I was very fond of the actors who were playing my children. I asked Ken where my lines were and he said there were none.

He said that, on the word 'Action!', he just wanted me to run around the corner and let my emotions take over and keep thinking about those kids. With that single word – and the click of the clapperboard – I took off.

My reaction as I turned that street corner was exactly what Ken was looking for. I fell into character immediately; my jaw dropped at the action unfolding in front of me, and all I could think of was those kids.

There were fire engines and ambulances everywhere and smoke billowing out of the window of the flat where we were supposed to be living. Everything seemed so real, so it was all too easy to become caught up in the drama. I ran forward, desperately trying to get to the flat. Then, as I tried to get through the police barrier, people were stopping me. Why are they stopping me? I thought. They're my kids and I want to find them. I was almost fighting with them, desperately trying to make them understand it was my flat and that my kids were inside. By now my adrenalin was bubbling. The police told me the kids had been hurt and bundled me into a panda car before it sped to the hospital. Every word, every movement was improvised. I knew exactly what that word meant now.

What I saw next frightened the shit out of me. If I thought the scene at the burning flat was realistic, nothing prepared me for what I saw when I walked on to the hospital set. I still hadn't been given any lines or any instructions. Ken just sat in the background patiently, as the cameras tracked every flicker of emotion and every crease of anguish on my face. When I saw the little boy who played my oldest boy Shaun, I let out this hideous scream and of course the cameras kept on rolling. I had never seen make-up like that before; it looked so authentic I really thought something serious had happened to those children. Then I remembered it was all fake. The make-up artists had excelled themselves; God knows how long it had taken them. I have replayed that scene over and over again on DVD. It carries the hallmark of a genius... A genius called Ken Loach.

Working with Ken was great therapy for me. He took me under his wing, played to my strengths and understood my weaknesses. If Ken had not been a director, he could have made a wonderful psychologist or therapist. He is a very deep, caring man who has the utmost compassion for all he does and believes in the people he works with. I will be forever grateful to him for the chance he gave me and his belief in me that never wavered. *Ladybird Ladybird* exorcised every demon I had.

CHAPTER TWENTY

AWARDS

Tears for Jean

I looked at its face the morning they told me you were dead
How I wanted all the clock hands to go back so you'd be with me instead
Oh, Auntie Jean, I did not know that day was the day you'd die
And ot all the cruel places fate chose a cold roadside
In my mind I've gone through a thousand times why I didn't pick you up
The guilt, pain and anger messes my head up
And when I awake each morning I pray to the Lord up above
That you are in heaven's garden where I send all my love

I so enjoyed working on *Ladybird Ladybird* with my first screen partner Ray Winstone. Ray was a seasoned actor and, unlike me, knew what he was doing. He played the part of Simon, a bully and wife-beater, and so would have to beat me up. Ray would always apologise before and after each scene where he beat me. He explained that he had trained as a professional boxer and he could time each punch to perfection, so that he could pull back at exactly the right moment. I trusted him completely. I left it all to him and he showed me how to roll with the punches.

I remember watching those scenes at the premiere. They looked so real and believable. I would be lying if I said they weren't harrowing for me as they did bring back some pretty horrific memories of the abuse I had suffered at the hands of my first husband. However, what I really appreciated was the contrast Ken Loach captured between the two men that played my screen lovers. Ray played the monster and Vladimir Vega (who played Jorge) the complete opposite. It was so beautiful, like watching fire and water.

Contrary to what I was expecting, I didn't seem to be making a fool of myself during filming. On the first Friday afternoon of the shoot, I was called into the office on the set. I was a little scared. I thought I was going to get the sack or at least some sort of bollocking, though I couldn't think why. When I got there, a lady presented me with an envelope and I asked her what it was.

She looked at me as if I was daft. 'Your wages,' she said with a grin.

You may think that this is hard to believe but I'd never even asked about wages up until then. I didn't know how much I was getting paid or when I was getting anything, I was just happy that I felt I was coping with the role of Maggie.

There was a cheque in the envelope for £1,000. I thanked the lady and walked out.

The following week, I was called back to the same office again. This time I really did think I was getting sacked. She handed me another cheque for £1,000.

'There's been a mistake,' I said. 'I got my money last week.'

She looked up and smiled. 'You get this every week, Crissy.'

I was there for eight weeks and sure enough an envelope was handed over every Friday. It was more money than I'd seen in my life. I felt like a millionaire.

Ken Loach's compassion and understanding of life shone throughout the shoot. Ken is a model professional and doesn't like anyone in the actor's eye line. The only people who see the scenes are the cameramen and the sound engineers; everyone else is banned from the set apart from the actors who are taking part. Therefore, even the lead actors have no real idea where the film is actually heading. Yes, of course, we have an idea as to what type of film it is, but until we all sit down at the premiere we really don't know how the many weeks of filming are going to fit together. That's Ken's job, of course. Ken rarely looked at anybody doing the shots; normally, he would sit in a corner looking at the floor, his eyes glued to it constantly. Ken's ears are his eyes and the camera his soul; it all comes together wonderfully well, almost like magic.

Towards the end of the shoot's second month, we spent hours on just one scene where Vladimir and I were shouting at each other. We shouted and screamed at each other on the verge of coming to blows before sliding down a wall holding hands. We went over the scene again and again and eventually Ken said he was happy with it. Once he said that, he started clapping, as did the sound engineers and cameramen. Vladimir and I looked at each other, as if to say, 'What?'

Ken smiled. 'That's it,' he said. 'We're finished. It's a WRAP: Wind Reel And Print.'

'What?' I repeated.

'The film's finished,' he replied.

There were lots of tears that evening as we celebrated with a few drinks in a local pub because everyone was like a real big happy family. Saying goodbye was hard for me because, unlike your real family, I never knew when or if I would see those faces again. It was early November 1993 when the shooting finished, and I walked out with my belongings into the cold London night and got on a train back to Liverpool to get on with my life.

The £8,000 I earned was banked and the first thing I did

was pay off my catalogue bill which had run to quite a few hundred pounds. I bought a three-piece suite too, the first one that didn't belong to someone else first. I went over the top spending £800 on a leather Chesterfield. I remember the day it was delivered, I felt so proud that I was actually able to pay for it, and when I sat down in it that evening, watching the TV with Hayley and Tracy either side of me, I never wanted to get up. I don't remember what was on TV, I was lost in my own thoughts. I'd made it, I'd finally made it; things were going to be different from now on.

I went to town on the girls. I bought them everything I thought they needed and spent a small fortune on leather coats for the winter, new beds, and I bought them a gold necklace each. The only people who had gold when I was growing up were the moneylenders. That Christmas was the best ever with more presents than would fit under the tree. I didn't care, my darling girls had gone without for too long and now I was making up for it.

While I was out shopping the week before Christmas, I decided to buy Tom something really special. He'd been a little bit distant lately and I suppose a little depressed. It would also be his birthday in January, and I figured that the present was a little extravagant but justified it, thinking that it could double up as his birthday present as well. Tom just got a card on Christmas morning but, when he opened it, a holiday voucher fell into his lap. It was a two-week all-inclusive break to Barbados; finally we were going abroad on holiday together. We were off to paradise.

The holiday, unfortunately, was a disaster. It gave Tom the opportunity to drink 24 hours a day and in the middle of the holiday I thought he'd died as he slept off the effects of an eight-hour binge on rum. He slept non-stop for nearly 48 hours. I couldn't wake him but let him sleep because at least he wasn't drinking. When he woke up, I begged him to stop drinking and get some help when we got home. He refused both requests. He said, 'Shut up, I'm on holiday and I'm entitled to get drunk.'

He continued drinking for the rest of the holiday and on the 11-hour flight back to Britain. I tried desperately to sleep but my mind was racing and wouldn't allow it. When had all this started to go wrong? I wondered. I began to blame myself as Tom hadn't drunk this much when I first met him. As I stepped off the plane at Manchester Airport, I felt drained. As soon as I walked through the door at noon, I took a phone call asking me to do a gig that night. The £8,000 was rapidly diminishing, I couldn't refuse work and, anyway, what better way to block out Tom's problems than to get back on the stage and throw myself into my stand-up routine?

Three days later, I had a gig in Stoke-on-Trent and rang Auntie Jean up to see if she wanted to come. Uncle Joey, Jean's husband, told me she'd gone out but shouldn't be too long. She hadn't called by the time I pulled out of the drive. I noticed Tom waving out of the window as I pushed the car into gear. I thought he was just waving me off, but later I found out he was waving to attract my attention, to tell me that Auntie Jean was on the phone and wanted to come to work with me. Because I missed the call, Auntie Jean had gone to her daughter-in-law's house to see young Stephen.

On her journey home, a car sped around the corner and ploughed into her. She was killed almost instantly, and was pronounced dead on arrival at the hospital.

I was inconsolable and I blamed myself for months afterwards. If only I'd done that differently, if only I'd stopped to see what Tom wanted, if only I hadn't been in such a rush. If, if, if… It took me a long time to come to terms with Auntie Jean's death, and I still find it hard to this day. It was like losing my mother all over again.

* * *

It was late January 1994 when I got a phone call to say I was needed in London for the premiere of *Ladybird Ladybird* in Soho. It was a magical evening and I couldn't believe it was me on a film screen as I relaxed in the plush seats of the cinema. It was all a bit unreal at first because I had never ever dreamed that I would be playing a part in a real film. Everyone was so complimentary afterwards and it was great to catch up with the team again. I was informed that the film had been entered for the prestigious Berlin Film Festival. I was also told that I had been chosen by the film company to promote the film in Berlin and after the awards.

'What does that involve?' I asked.

It meant that I would be flown first-class all over the world and stay in the finest hotels. A stranger in a nice suit from the film company told me my career was only just beginning. He said it was the opportunity of a lifetime to put myself in the shop window and what was even better was that it wouldn't cost me a penny to promote myself. Would I do it? How could I refuse?

My first trip to Berlin was absolutely amazing. I was picked up at the airport by a chauffeur complete with an expensive-looking suit and peaked cap. He walked me to the biggest black stretch limousine I'd ever seen and, although I tried to remain composed, he saw right through my amazement. He opened the door of the vehicle and in perfect English said, 'Have you never been in a posh car before?'

'Of course I have,' I replied. 'I've been to loads of funerals.'

AWARDS

The hotel was out of this world. I'd never seen anything like it, five stars and wall-to-wall millionaires strolling around the foyer. I went to the desk and said to the receptionist I thought there had been a mistake and that maybe I had been sent to the wrong hotel.

When I gave my name, she snapped her fingers. A little man in a blue suit appeared and the receptionist ordered him to take me to my suite. I bent down to get my bag and it was gone.

'Someone's robbed me bag,' I shouted as the receptionist smiled calmly.

She pointed over to the lift where Mr Blue Suit stood, holding my bag. 'The porter will take your bag, Miss Rock,' she said with a smile.

Did I feel small! I wanted the ground to open up and swallow me.

I was taken up to the top floor and the porter opened the door to my room – only it wasn't a room; it was a suite. It contained a bed which seemed to be the size of a tennis court. 'How many people are staying here?' I said. 'I can't share a bed like that, I'm a married woman.'

I walked into the room and it opened up to a lounge overlooking the city with a balcony that seemed as big as our garden at home.

'This is just for me?' I asked.

'Yes.' He smiled. 'All for you, Madam.'

Everything in the bathroom was marble or granite with matching gold taps in the sink and bath. Even the bidet had a gold plughole and the bath seemed as spacious as a swimming pool. In the lounge was a huge sofa and television and it opened up on to a smaller room with a desk and writing paper and pens with the logo and name of the hotel. My God... my room was like a huge apartment and I was terrified to touch anything because everything was so beautiful and expensive, so I just sat there in the chair and took it all in. I must be dreaming, I thought. I couldn't believe it.

When the phone rang in my room, it made me jump. I presumed it was reception, having realised that they'd put me in the wrong room. But it wasn't; it was Sally Hibbin, the film's producer, to tell me that she was waiting downstairs with Ken. We were off to the cinema for a private viewing of *Ladybird Ladybird*.

After the showing of the film, I was whisked through a door where a sight awaited me that I will never forget for the rest of my life. There were literally hundreds of people in the room, television cameras and huge microphones, and at least two hundred photographers with cameras flashing. Others were applauding and cheering; people were calling my name and asking me questions. I was overwhelmed and I could feel my eyes welling up with tears because I just couldn't believe it. Ken looked at me with his lovely smile and I was lost for words.

How could all this be happening to me? I am nobody. A working-class girl from Liverpool 8. Things like this shouldn't happen to working-class girls from Liverpool 8. Liverpool 8 to international superstardom. Was it all a dream and when was I going to wake up?

A wake-up call of sorts happened the next day. I was flown home, and, when I got home, Tom told me I had a gig in Carlisle the following evening. He smelled terribly of booze. I could smell it on his breath; it seeped through the pores in his skin. But I said nothing about it.

After my performance in Carlisle, the concert secretary told me I had to call home urgently. My heart was in my mouth. I was afraid to ring home as my thoughts drifted back to that awful night when I had to ring home and was told that Auntie Jean had died. I couldn't do it, so, God love him, the concert secretary did it for me. All Tom told him was that I was to come home straight away.

I was hysterical thinking the worst possible thing had happened, that something had happened to Tracy or Hayley. I couldn't even begin to think about driving, I was shaking like a leaf, and eventually the concert secretary and his friend hatched a plan. His friend drove my car and the concert secretary drove his following on behind, and between them they took me all the way back to Liverpool. How kind was that? Despite the shit I've been through at the hands of others, I'm constantly being reminded that there are still many pearls in the human race. God forgive me, I still can't remember their names but they know who they are. Thank you from the bottom of my heart.

When I walked through the door at 28 Croxdale Road, Tom had something to tell me. He announced we were both off to Berlin. 'There's a car picking us up at eight o'clock in the morning,' he said with a smile. 'It's taking us to the airport.'

I could have hit him. Why couldn't he have just said that on the phone and saved me three hours of anguish?

The following morning, we were taken to Manchester Airport. When we got to the check-in for the Berlin flight, we were given a gold envelope containing two VIP tickets. When we landed at Berlin Airport, for some mysterious reason, we were whisked through the formalities of Customs and passport control. Then I couldn't help noticing that there were press and film cameras everywhere. Like a pair of dopes, we were looking to see who had landed. 'Is it the Queen or someone really famous?' I asked Tom.

What I didn't realise was that the press were there for me.

I answered a few questions and posed for some photographs, all the time wondering what all the fuss was about. After 20 minutes, our driver appeared in another huge stretch limo and we were taken to another five-star hotel in the centre of Berlin. We'd barely unpacked our things when we received a phone call from reception to say that a car would be picking us up in an hour and taking us to the awards ceremony of the Berlin Film Festival.

The award ceremony was unbelievable, and so unreal. The press people were out in force and focusing on the big stars who had flown in from London and Hollywood. My eyes nearly popped out of their sockets when Sophia Loren's name was called out for a lifetime achievement award and she rose just a few seats away from me. She was absolutely stunning, oozing class, and I remember her neck was like a graceful swan. She didn't walk to the stage, she glided.

The compère then announced the award for best actress for the 1994 Silver Bear at the International Berlin Film Festival. He read out four nominees: Joanne Woodward, Isabella Rossellini, Emma Thompson and Crissy Rock.

'What the f...!' T and I just looked at each other in amazement. It was the first I knew that I'd even been nominated, which at least exorcised all my fears about making a fool of myself during filming. I thought we were just at the awards ceremony to have a Kia-Ora, some popcorn and go home. But what happened next was simply unbelievable: the compère tore open the envelope and announced the winner's name: Crissy Rock.

Crissy Rock from Liverpool 8? Fucking hell... that's me!

The applause was deafening. I could hardly even get up from my seat because my legs were shaking so much. It seemed to take forever to get to the stage. I seemed to just float there. The cameramen were on their feet and the flashbulbs blinded me, slowing me up even more. Was I just dreaming or was it real? I stood on stage in my £9.99 Bon Marche cardigan and a black dress my friend had lent me, holding a Silver Bear award that was probably worth more than the whole of Croxdale Road. Apart from my wedding ring, it was the only other piece of silver I had ever had.

The next winner to reach the stage was Tom Hanks, best actor for his role in *Philadelphia*.

The rest of the evening was a blur. I don't think I even had time for a couple of glasses of champagne as question after question was fired at me from reporters around the world. Even after that awards ceremony in Berlin, everything went crazy. I would get phone calls in the middle of the night from Australia and America, New Zealand and Japan requesting interviews that would be transmitted on television and radio stations.

CHAPTER TWENTY ONE

LIVING LIKE A STAR

With throats unslaked, with black lips baked,
Agape they heard me call:
Gramercy! they for joy did grin,
And all at once their breath drew in,
As they were drinking all.

Suddenly, promoting *Ladybird Ladybird* took over my life. The film company flew me all over the world. It was as if every week a set of flight tickets would arrive: America, Germany, Italy, France. I'd get the tickets, study the dates then phone my agency to cancel the relevant stand-up gigs I had been booked to do. I never asked the film company about expenses and wages but assumed they'd surely replace the money I'd be losing.

Those first few trips were out of this world. Although I was a little lonely on my own in strange countries, a driver would always collect me at the airport and I'd be transported to the best hotels and booked into the best rooms. I'd attend press conferences, do interviews for television and radio, and be treated like a VIP. I'd eat in the hotel restaurants or sometimes just have canapés at a TV studio, and the film company was right: it didn't cost me a penny. Even so, there was no mention of expenses, or any indication that the money I was losing from my work as a comic would be reimbursed. I put it to the back of my mind, thinking they would settle everything afterwards. There'd be an envelope waiting for me back home, maybe even at the end of the tour. After all, they'd paid well enough when we were filming.

And still the flight tickets continued to drop on to the doormat and I'd be off at a minute's notice, staying in luxury hotels around the globe. One night I would be in Paris, the next day in Norway, then I'd be whisked off to America for two or three days, and it was always the same: press interviews and every journalist asking the same question as their international colleagues had asked the day before. Unfortunately, fortune never came with fame. It was like winning the lottery but without having the money. I still hadn't received a penny – and yet I wouldn't have missed it for the world.

I also seemed to be picking up awards for fun. I won a best actress award at the Chicago Film Festival, a Spanish National Radio award for a foreign actress, the French Henri Langlois Prize and picked up three category awards at the Hamburg and Dresden International Festivals, as well as an award closer to home at the London International Film Festival.

Back home I was brought back down to earth again – realising that Tom's drinking was getting worse, and having to commit to at least five gigs a week just to cover the bills. I was more than a little upset that the £8,000 from *Ladybird Ladybird* had long gone, and I estimated I'd lost at least twice that amount through turning down work in favour of globetrotting promotion ventures for the film company. Tom was throwing it in my face as the bills started to pile up but it seemed easy enough to take out a loan or apply for a credit card. After all, I was Crissy Rock, award-winning actress, and the bank managers surely knew it was just a matter of time before the next big cheque fell through the letter box. I guess the bank managers were right; they knew what they were doing.

Roger my comedy agent had taken me as far as he could, so he got in touch with an agent called Kenneth Earle. Kenneth was a little eccentric perhaps, but a pure gentleman. He got me good acting roles but I continued with my bread-and-butter comedy act and the gigs. I was luckier than most working actresses in that I didn't have to sit by the phone waiting for it to ring.

I'd been offered a part in *Peak Practice*, the ITV drama. Its director, Alan Grint, was the man who turned me into a regular working actress. Working on that was cold but fun. It was like a dream. Now I was working alongside people I had only ever seen on television, like Amanda Burton and Kevin Whately.

After that, I did *Dalziel and Pascoe* with Warren Clarke and Colin Buchanan. I played a housekeeper, Annie Greave, who was murdered and then dumped in Epping Forest. Only it wasn't Epping Forest, and, of course, I wasn't really dead. It was about seven o'clock in the morning and they made me up to look like the bride of Dracula, saying, 'Lie there and don't move.'

I couldn't move, not with 10 years of undergrowth and nettles sticking up my backside.

In 1996, when I secured a contract for *Brazen Hussies* – a feature-length TV drama for the BBC with Julie Walters and Robert Lindsay – I was promised my biggest pay cheque to date: £32,000. Nice money, but let's just say that I never received anywhere near that sort of money in the end. Tom's eyes were dazzled with the possible pound signs. He wanted to move house, figuring out that an actress who was working with Julie Walters deserved better. 'You wouldn't see Julie Walters living on a council estate,' he would say.

Who was he kidding? I wasn't in the same league as Julie, I told him, and, anyway, I loved living on the council estate.

But he wanted a change and suggested we buy a house. I confess, I liked the sound of it and thought that it might give Tom a new interest in life instead of just drinking. Eventually, I gave in, and put a deposit on a property in Croxteth Country Park. Tom had convinced me that it was affordable and it was time to move to a better standard of accommodation. I took all my wage slips from my agency as well as details of my contract from *Brazen Hussies* and the bank couldn't wait to throw money at me. Number 10 Sherwood Court was a modern town house and it even had a car port. Posh or what?

It was beautiful and, yes, on the face of it, I loved our new house, but I started to have doubts on the day we moved, as I walked round our old house from room to room, thinking about all the memories there. I remembered the times when we'd sat with no money, no heating, no electric, when we'd pretended to the kids it was all a big game. I looked at the growth lines I'd drawn on the door frame measuring Tracy's and Hayley's progress. As I walked down the path of my council house for the last time, I knew in my heart I was making an enormous mistake. My neighbours were my best friends, and, as I recalled the joy and laughter we'd shared, it broke my heart that I was leaving all this behind.

I walked down the path in tears as some of my neighbours waved me off. Tom looked at me as if I was stupid. Get a grip, I told myself, and tried to convince myself how beautiful the house was at Croxteth Country Park, with new carpets and curtains and – for the first time in my life – a fitted kitchen. I deserved it, I thought to myself. I was entitled to it for all the hard work I'd put in and the sacrifices I had made. The house would be a turning point. I'd spend more time at home and Tom would get his life back... I hoped.

Not long after we moved into Croxteth Park, I got a call from the taxman inviting me for an interview in the local office. From the moment I walked into the office, I knew they were after my blood. I wasn't worried though, as I had always made a point of paying tax on everything I received by way of income, even the cash-in-hand jobs. The official couldn't comprehend how little I'd actually earned over a two-year period. He had a list of everything I'd been in and of course the details of my year away promoting *Ladybird Ladybird*. He wouldn't have it that I hadn't received a penny in income or expenses; he simply wouldn't believe it. He pushed a slip of paper across the desk. At the bottom was the figure: £46,751.

When I asked what it was, he said it was the calculation of how much extra tax I had to pay. I nearly fell off the seat laughing before I realised he was deadly serious. He'd plucked the figure from thin air; there wasn't an ounce of logic in the figures he'd used to assess the tax. After several meetings with my accountant and officials from the Inland Revenue, they got the figure down to less than half the original assessment. I wouldn't pay it, and in fact I couldn't pay it. My accountant said I had no choice: it had to be paid or I would be going to jail. In the end, she set me up on a plan where I had to pay back nearly £500 per month for five years. It left a bitter taste in my mouth but thankfully the work coming in just about covered what I had to pay out.

The work was creatively rewarding too. Working with Julie Walters on *Brazen Hussies* was an honour, because, being a comic, she was my idol. She was not only great fun to work with, but a lovely genuine person. As well as Robert Lindsay, my other co-stars on the film were Alun Armstrong and Julian Clary. Julian parades around as camp as a tent but off-screen he is the loveliest, gentlest man you could ever meet.

It was during that shoot that I found out my youngest daughter Hayley was pregnant. She was only 15 at the time and I was devastated, as I feared she was making the same mistakes I had made. Also, I felt guilty that I had not been at home to support her as much as I should have been. The day I heard the news, we were filming an emotional scene for the film. My character's husband, played by Robert, had been caught with his girlfriend (Julie Walters). My instruction from the director was 'to lose it' and start smashing up the furniture, put some feeling into it. I really went for it that day, with my emotions taking over, and I took the cheap chipboard furniture apart as if it were origami. As I finished the take, I was congratulated on my acting from several quarters. Some were even applauding. But I wasn't acting that day.

I tried to pretend that Hayley's pregnancy wasn't happening. Work can be a great escape and I had more than my fair share. But you couldn't turn the clock back, and eventually, thank God, I came to my senses and told Hayley that I would stand by her whatever she chose to do. As Hayley's baby grew inside her, I secretly shed more than a few tears, but, one month before her 16th birthday, she gave birth to a little girl that she named Melissa. When I looked at my beautiful granddaughter, I melted like an ice cream on an August afternoon and all the anxiety attacks, all the tears and worries and concerns, disappeared in an instant. I would sit by her cot and look at her for hours thinking how perfect she was. I would sing to her, 'You are my sunshine, my only sunshine,' and she'd laugh and giggle, blowing little tiny bubbles that I'd wipe away with a paper tissue.

She was such a good baby and hardly ever cried. She went to sleep smiling and woke up the same way. I have four granddaughters now. Danielle was next to be born, then Caitlyn, and the youngest is Ashley. Each and every one of them brings me so much joy. Each has their own little personalities.

By the late nineties, Tracy and Hayley had both moved out of Sherwood Court, and my busy schedule and money in the bank gave Tom the perfect platform to continue ruining his life – though that's not the way he would have seen it at the time. Meanwhile, my acting roles continued. In 1999, I starred in *Dockers*, written by Jimmy McGovern, and which also featured Ricky Tomlinson. Once more, Ricky and I got on like a house on fire, and the jokes were flying, both on- and off-screen. However, I will remember that film with particular fondness because my granddaughters Danielle and Caitlyn played small parts in it too. I still watch their scenes on the DVD of the film that's under my television at home.

In 1998, I had also toured Britain in the play *Shellfish*. We spent a month rehearsing and went all over the country taking the play to the masses. It was in Richmond that I met Lynda La Plante. Lynda and her sister came to see the play and loved it. She invited me to dinner after the show and we have remained good friends ever since.

When Lynda had a book launch at the Ritz, she invited me along. As I stood behind her, and watched her signing some books for people, a man approached me. He was wearing a hideous blue suit with oversized lapels, a dicky bowtie and a fedora hat. He spoke with marbles in his mouth.

'Hello, dear, are you a literist too?'

'Oh no,' I said proudly, 'I can read and write perfectly now.'

As I watched Lynda, I was thinking how fantastic it must be to be able to write a book and get it published. After that book launch, I began scribbling and making notes and dared to dream just a little bit about a book. They say there's a good book in everyone. Surely not me, though? I had only just started to read as an adult and my spelling and grammar were atrocious.

In general, my working life could not have been going any better. At home, behind the closed doors of 10 Sherwood Court, it was a living nightmare. A pattern was beginning to emerge, not a pattern that satisfied me. Tom was now drinking around the clock, simply topping up his alcohol intake. Our marital bed had all but gone, with Tom choosing to make his bed on the settee. He would drink, sleep, wake up on the same settee, have a cup of tea and then start drinking again. The routine never changed. If ever I complained, he would get abusive. 'Fuckin' shut up,' he would say. 'Fuck your house, fuck you and your kids, that's why I'm drinking.' Tom would blame his drinking on anyone and anything. He blamed Tracy and Hayley, and then just Hayley when Tracy moved out. After Hayley moved out, it was me or the bills, the house, his family, my family, any family, the taxman, the bank… anyone. I now know this is typical of an alcoholic but at the time I didn't. Eventually, I started to believe in what he was saying, and started to blame myself. Tom was a zombie, drinking, sleeping, drinking, sleeping, and never moving from his favourite position on the settee. I'd leave him at twelve, come in at two, three, six or eleven and still he'd be in the same position I had left him in hours earlier, only with a dozen empty beer cans lying on the floor next to him.

My only way of coping was by immersing myself in work

and trying to improve myself. I even enrolled on an art course. For 12 months, I attended the course regularly, as it meant I had another night away from the house. At the end of that year, there was an exam, which, if I did well, resulted in a qualification. I studied hard in the weeks leading up to the exam, but, on the day itself, it was raining cats and dogs. I finished my shift at work and got home with an hour to spare before the test. For once, Tom wasn't incoherent. My car was in the garage and as Tom's car wasn't an automatic I couldn't legally drive it so I asked him to run me to the bus stop which was about a mile away. He could see how hard it was raining but turned round and told me to walk. He went to the fridge and took out a can of lager. I couldn't believe what he'd just done and, all of a sudden, there seemed to be no point to the exam. I just kicked off my shoes, went upstairs, lay down on the bed and cried myself to sleep.

Tom had changed from the man I married, his illness had taken over. He didn't care, showed no affection and just drank and drank and drank. Things had to come to a head and I was more than a little concerned that I wasn't getting as many comedy gigs as I used to. As the bills continued to pile up, it was during a heated argument that Tom made a bizarre suggestion – that we should move house again. I agreed; after all, the memories of Sherwood Court were not exactly pleasant ones.

We moved to a house in Whiston, at 47 Copperwood Drive. Again, the bank was only too happy to increase the mortgage. Tom even moderated his drinking for a few weeks and I honestly thought that he'd turned a corner. He hadn't been drinking or been abusive, and things were running along smoothly. I was a little worried at the £1,000 that went on interest and endowment payments every month but figured that, if Tom could just cut down on his alcoholic grocery bill, we could just about keep our heads above water.

The majority of my money was coming from acting jobs, which was all very well but, as any actor will tell you, it's not a regular income. Furthermore, the phone calls from the agency advising me where and when I would be performing were becoming less frequent. I was lucky if I was getting one gig a week. The working men's clubs were going out of fashion, it seemed, particularly with the younger generation. I noticed clubs in Liverpool closing, boarding up their windows or getting turned into doctor's surgeries or disco bars. All of a sudden, sitting in a club listening to a singer or a comedian seemed to be old hat and the youngsters would just flock to the Liverpool city-centre bars instead.

With the gigs drying up, I took a position as a care worker just to make ends meet. Why had I taken on such a big mortgage and why did those credit-card bills seem to be getting bigger each month? And, of course, on top of that, there was the £500 taxman payment. I tried to reason with Tom, begging him to get a job, but he told me that, with the money I was making, why should he? He was living in Cloud Cuckoo Land. I showed him all the reminder letters and final demands, but he pushed them back at me and told me to deal with it. His drinking increased again, and in no time he was back into zombie mode.

At times I could hardly sleep wondering where the next penny was coming from and praying that the next big job was just around the corner. One night, I was lying awake trying to work out such mental calculations when I became aware that Tom was moving around downstairs. I heard a few doors banging and a noise as if he'd fallen over. Sleep wouldn't come so I went down to investigate.

Tom was sitting on the settee with a large tumbler of water. He looked like shit. He was shaking and sweating and could hardly hold the glass.

'What is it, Tom?' I asked, concerned. 'What's wrong?'

He looked at me like a two-week-old puppy, but with lost, soulless eyes.

'What's wrong?' I repeated. I took his empty glass. 'Let me get you another water. Tell me, are you ill?'

Tom handed me the glass. 'It's not water, Crissy,' he whispered, his voice all croaky. 'It's vodka… I'm sorry.'

Tom told me he had been drinking vodka throughout the night for about six months. He was in far deeper than I ever imagined but now he surely couldn't deny he had a serious problem.

Yet he did. I sat with him for over an hour begging him to get help. I looked through the Yellow Pages, found the page for Alcoholics Anonymous and wrote the number down on a piece of paper that I pressed into his hand. He kept shaking his head and told me to stop nagging him. He even blamed my nagging for turning him to drink.

'You're drinking neat vodka at three in the morning,' I yelled at him. 'How can't you see you have a problem?'

But Tom just curled up on the settee and went to sleep. Tom never came up to the marital bed again; the settee became his bed. He'd drink, fall asleep, wake up and start drinking again. Most of the time, he was incoherent and could hardly string a sentence together. At other times, when he was capable of speaking, it would always be abusive and he'd blame everything on me.

I came home one day after a long shift at work. Tom was sleeping on the settee, 12 empty cans of lager lay at his feet, and what I presumed was his last can lying on its side with lager seeping all over the carpet. I couldn't take much more. I stepped over the cans and went into the kitchen to make myself a coffee. I was lost, absolutely helpless. I'd tried calling the AA but they told me it would need to be Tom who called. What could I do if he wasn't prepared to help himself? I'd tried every approach in the book. I'd yelled and I'd begged, I'd cried and pleaded with him. I'd told him I loved him. I'd told him I hated him. I'd even threatened him with divorce.

Exasperated and exhausted, I left him for three days, packed my clothes in a suitcase and stayed with a friend. When I got back, he hadn't even realised I'd been away, each day blending into the next one. I refused to buy beer and refused to give him any money but he would always find a way to feed his addiction or I would cave in. Nothing mattered to him, just the next can of beer. During one heated argument, I even feigned a heart attack just to try to get him to take me seriously. We were shouting at each other when I felt a slight pain in my chest. I think I probably strained a muscle and what seemed like a good idea at the time came to me. I threw myself on the floor clutching at my chest pretending I couldn't breathe. His reaction? He stepped over me, walked to the fridge and took out a can of lager. He stepped over me again on the way back to the settee.

The day I threw a cup of coffee over him will stick with me for the rest of my life. The post lay on the doormat as I opened the front door. More red letters. I threw them on the pile with the others. I'd almost given up and now I was behind with the mortgage too. I stepped over him as I walked into the lounge. He'd fallen from the settee and was lying in the middle of the floor. I stood in the kitchen with my coffee looking out of the window and wondering how it had come to this.

He walked through and spoke. 'Don't ask if I want one, will you.'

His breath stank of stale beer; he started poking me in the chest.

'Self, self, self,' he said. 'Don't think of me, don't ask me if I want one.'

I snapped. 'You want a coffee?' I asked. 'Here, have mine.'

I wanted to freeze the moment as the scalding hot coffee flew through the air. I wanted to rewind the tape but of course I couldn't. The hot coffee hit him in the chest. Thank God he had a thick jumper on and he wasn't badly scalded. But I wasn't done yet. I completely lost it. I screamed at him to get out of the house but he calmly took off the steaming jumper, threw it on the kitchen floor and went back to his favourite spot on the settee. I followed him through to the living room, effing and blinding at him at the top of my voice.

'Can't you see what you're doing to us, you drunken bastard?'

Tom was completely ignoring my rant. I was like the exorcist possessed as he sat on the settee and smirked. I grabbed the Yellow Pages and opened it up at the AA page. I picked up the phone and dialled the number. I was still screaming at Tom when a man answered.

'Hello, my name's Roger and I'm an alcoholic.'

'So is he.' I pointed at Tom, screaming down the phone, and believe me I was screaming. I think the pictures on the wall were rattling. 'Get him out of my house before I fucking kill him.'

As I was ranting down the phone about how much Tom was drinking and ruining our lives, Roger was as calm as a cucumber. 'What's your name?' he asked.

'Crissy.'

'Are you an alcoholic?'

'No, my husband is though – and he's a fucking prick and I want him out.'

'I can't speak to you, Crissy, you'll have to put your husband on.'

I looked at Tom and held out the phone. 'Speak to him.'

Tom shook his head.

'Speak to him, you prick,' I shouted even louder. I felt really sorry for Roger on the other end.

Tom could see how determined I was as I continued to stand with the phone shouting, 'Speak, you bastard!' I must have tried to persuade him at least a dozen times.

Eventually, he stood up and took the phone. I remember the conversation word for word; Tom even put on a posh telephone voice.

'Hello, yes, my name's Tom... no, I haven't got a drink problem... yes, I like a drink... no, I'm not drunk now and this is what I have to put up with every day.'

And finally: 'No, I'm not prepared to do anything about it. I'm fine, thank you. I don't need your help, thanks.' And with that he pressed the end button on the phone and went back to the settee.

I went upstairs to the bathroom, sank to the floor and the tears I'd fought for so long flowed like a river.

A few days later, the phone rang. It was a lady from Al-Anon, a support group for the families and friends of alcoholics. She was called Cathy and explained that Roger had passed my number on. The first thing she said was: 'You do realise he's ill, don't you?'

Cathy asked me where I lived and told me there was an Al-Anon meeting near us the following evening. She sounded so sweet that I agreed to go. The meeting was in a church in Dragon Lane and I was very nervous as I walked up the path. I was a few minutes late and the meeting had already started. It took all my courage but I walked in and sat in a seat near the back.

The lady addressing everyone noticed me and after a few minutes welcomed the newcomer to the meeting.

'What's your name, dear?' she asked.

'Crissy.'

'Welcome, Crissy, and please tell me how long you have had a weight problem.'

A weight problem? I was seven stone wet through. Shit, I'd stumbled into the local Weight Watchers meeting.

I couldn't even get to the right bloody meeting. I made my apologies and left, bursting into tears as I got outside. I sat crying on the wall for five minutes, and felt that the whole world was against me. An elderly man and woman appeared and asked me what was wrong. I blurted out that I was going to an Al-Anon meeting but must have got mixed up with the night. They introduced themselves as Dave and Cathy and said I hadn't got the wrong night: the Al-Anon meeting was upstairs. They took me by the hand and led me through the door.

I went to Al-Anon every week for years and Dave became my sponsor, someone I could ring and speak to 24 hours a day. I sincerely believe Dave and Al-Anon saved my sanity. But during that long period, there was only one occasion where I managed to persuade Tom to attend an Alcoholics Anonymous meeting.

He walked out halfway through.

CHAPTER TWENTY TWO

MONEY'S TOO TIGHT TO MENTION

And those her ribs through which the sun
Did peer, as through a grate?
And is that Woman all her crew?
Is that a Death ? and are there two?
Is Death that Woman's mate?

The debt letters were piling up and I was six months behind with the mortgage. On the rare occasions Tom was sober I tried to tell him about our financial problems but he said it was my problem and I had to deal with it. I begged him to go out and find a job telling him that we couldn't rely on the acting or the comedy gigs. I was getting desperate even flying out to Benidorm in Spain every holiday I had, doing two or three gigs every night in a desperate attempt to keep the wolf from the door.

It was no good. Eventually, the bank took me to court. Although the house was in joint names Tom refused to go. I stood in the dock like a convicted criminal. I had four jobs: care worker, actress, earnings from UK comedy, and earnings from comedy work in Spain. How on earth had it come to this?

The judge spoke. 'Where exactly is your husband?'

I wanted to say, 'He's back home pissed, sir, that's the problem... Can't work, won't work and spends all of our money on enough drink to keep an army happy... And my head's absolutely cabbaged.'

I didn't. Instead, I told him the truth – that Tom was sick, though not the actual illness he was suffering from. I told him I couldn't go on much longer.

The judge was very fair as I explained my predicament and the hours I was working just to survive. I explained my five-year plan too and said I'd be able to make up the mortgage payments as soon as those payments were nearly at an end. I'd also put the house up for sale at a drastically reduced price but still the bank wanted to repossess it. The judge found in my favour and wouldn't let the bank repossess it. He made me pay two months' mortgage payment to the bank and I'd survived bankruptcy... just about. It seemed there was light at the end of the tunnel.

The day my five-year plan ended, I was called into the tax office. I genuinely thought they were going to congratulate me as I hadn't missed a single payment, but, with a straight face, the official announced that they were levying an interest charge for late payment.

'What late payment?' I asked. 'I've made every payment on time.'

The official told me I was five years late paying the tax, and so interest would be charged at the ridiculous rate of £20 per day over the five-year period. The figure was colossal, more than the original charge.

That was it. I threw the keys at him and told him to take the house. I'd given up.

'No, Ms Murray, wait, I'm sure...'

Cursing the system, I walked out. And on 25 August 2000, I was declared bankrupt.

I had the best night's sleep I'd had in a long time. Several months later, the house was sold. The Official Receiver took his share. He'd pay the taxman first (surprise, surprise) and then the banks. Tom was left with £27,000, and I got nothing because I was the one who'd been declared bankrupt. Life's a bitch, isn't it?

Tom swore again that he'd change his ways the day we moved out of the house in Whiston. But he didn't; he continued his old routine in our privately rented flat in St Helens. While I worked, he drank.

I loved my work in social services, loved my acting too, but I was truly in heaven when I was onstage doing my comedy. If life at home was a nightmare, I tolerated it, adopting the philosophy that three out of four parts of my life were great... so I should stop complaining and put up with it.

**

A few months after we had moved to St Helens, I visited the doctor, explaining a rather embarrassing condition that I had developed. Without examining me, he diagnosed thrush. I told him that I didn't think it was thrush because if I ate any more yoghurt I'd come into his surgery and start yodelling.

The doctor gave me some cream and sent me home. It didn't have any effect whatsoever and by now I had a burning sensation each time I went to the toilet.

I went to his surgery again. More cream and still no examination.

It took another 18 months before he referred me to a specialist. I arrived with a letter at a Well Woman clinic. A female doctor examined me. She was down between my legs for no more than 20 seconds.

'How long have you had this condition?' she asked.

'About two years,' I replied.

She shook her head. 'We need to take a biopsy immediately. We'll call an ambulance to take you there now.'

'I can't do it now,' I said. 'I'm working tonight.'

'No, you're not,' she said. 'You're not going anywhere.'

Within an hour they'd taken a biopsy. Foolishly, I told them I couldn't have a general anaesthetic as I had to work that night. Big mistake! It was simply the worst pain I have ever endured. In the end I vomited all over the poor nurse. I was in a terrible state, in floods of tears and with an excruciating pain that seemed never-ending. Incredibly, that evening I made it to work, even if my performance – on a stage somewhere in Manchester – was below-par.

Three weeks later, I was sitting in the clinic with the female doctor who had examined me. I'll never forget her face as I walked into the surgery. I knew that something was seriously wrong. She told me I had an abnormal pre-cancerous growth on my vagina and that the cells were white, indicating that they were on the move. White cells had been found on other parts of my vagina and my clitoris too. She described the growth as a mole, a mole with an open wound. When I peed, the urine had been getting into the wound causing the painful burning sensation.

She described my options. They could cut away the growth and hope it hadn't spread, though because they'd found white cells elsewhere there was a good chance that it had. Or I could have a partial vulvectomy which meant my clitoris and vaginal lips would be cut away and reconstructive surgery would take place.

It sounded a little harsh. I asked for her advice but she wouldn't commit herself. She then went on to describe the worst-case scenario: a full vulvectomy. A full vulvectomy would be performed if the cancerous cells spread. A full vulvectomy meant cutting away the whole vagina and leaving a hole inside me the size of a small melon. She described how the hole would need to be packed and the packing changed every six weeks because it would start to smell. A full vulvectomy would need to be performed if the cancer spread. The choice was clear. A partial vulvectomy would lessen the chance of the disease spreading and lessen the chances of that horrendous-sounding full vulvectomy and possibly even death.

I had a choice, but really I didn't have any choice at all.

They sent a Macmillan nurse called Sheila Judge to talk to me. Sheila reassured me and nothing was too much effort for her as she comforted me and answered all my questions openly and honestly. She told me that, with the advancement of modern medicines, more people lived with cancer than actually died. I talked to Sheila about the abuse I'd suffered as a child and we joked together as I said that my fanny had caused me nothing but trouble anyway. Once again, humour helped me to cope, helped me to keep my sanity, and having the ability to laugh and joke no matter what is what kept me going.

Sheila came to see me after the operation too. I told her it was all over. A part of my life had been cut away and I felt like a new person; I felt cleansed in a strange sort of way. My vagina was always something I'd been ashamed of.

Several weeks after the operation, I was sent to see a psychosexual therapist. She clearly hadn't read my notes, asking me if my problems were all in my head.

'No,' I replied. 'My problems were all in my clitoris but that's gone now.'

She turned red with embarrassment and realised why I was there. I wasn't some housewife with a hang-up about sex. I was there because my womanhood had been cut away by the surgeon's knife.

She started to ask the most incredible questions. I couldn't believe it when, a short while into the session, she asked, 'When was the last time you were aroused, Ms Murray?'

I had a sharp intake of breath. 'Yesterday.'

'Really... where?'

'On the settee watching *Countdown*. I've never managed to get the conundrum before.'

She spoke as if sex was the most important thing on the planet. I tried to explain to her that at that precise moment in time it was the last thing on my mind.

The next appointment arranged was with Tom, a joint therapy session. I tried to discuss it with him but he said he wouldn't go.

'Aren't you bothered if we never have sex again?' I asked him.

He thought for a few seconds and shrugged his shoulders. 'Not really,' he said.

I was dumbfounded, nearly speechless. 'And what about me?'

'What about you?' he replied.

Needless to say the appointment was never kept.

It's not over-dramatic to say I felt like a new person after the operation. It's difficult for me to describe but it was as if my life had taken on a new path. I felt trapped in St Helens and the work from acting had all but dried up, the nights on the road as a comic more or less gone. I spoke with my agent and told him about my plans to move to Benidorm where I more or less had been promised as much work as I wanted. He thought it was a good idea and I relished the thought of performing on a regular basis on stage, where I could be Crissy Rock.

I talked over my plans with Tom and he asked if he figured in them. Despite everything that had happened, I still loved him with all my heart and we cried as I told him that I wanted him to come, but that things would have to change. I wanted a new life, a new start. It wasn't too late, I told him, and I wanted my beautiful gentleman husband back, not a drunken, abusive beast.

Tom promised to give up drinking forever. I believed him, I really did.

We gave notice on the flat in St Helens and I flew to Benidorm to arrange my contracts and find accommodation. Benidorm is a drinkers' paradise and I paid the deposit on a rented house 10 miles from the town centre. I didn't want to put temptation in his way. A couple of weeks before Christmas in 2003, we flew out there to start our new life.

Tom lasted four days without a drink. On the fifth day, he went out for a walk at 11 in the morning and took a bus into Benidorm. He turned up in a taxi 18 hours later barely able to walk. He slept for a full 24 hours. He went out drinking again on Christmas Eve, and slept throughout Christmas Day as I ate my dinner on my own. This wasn't how it was supposed to be.

For three or four days after Christmas, he stalked round the house like a caged animal and on New Year's Eve he disappeared again before turning up two days later comatose. I gave him chance after chance over the next 11 months but made my mind up before Christmas 2004 that I wasn't going to spend a Christmas Day like the previous one.

I told him it was over. If I'd asked him to choose between me and the bottle, I'd have come a poor second.

I bought him a ticket home and gave him €3000, everything I had in the world. He seemed more than happy to go. It broke my heart that he was so casual about walking out of my life. He took the bus to Alicante Airport from Benidorm and a few days later I filed for divorce. It was the hardest thing I had ever done.

Leaving B had been easy; I hated everything about him and what he stood for. I hated what he had done to me and my daughters, the terror and misery he'd brought to our lives every single day.

Leaving Tom was so different. When Tom wasn't drunk, he was a gentleman, he was my rock, he'd been there for my daughters and given me the greatest gift I could ever have wished for when he helped me to start reading. I'd cast Tom adrift on his own and yet I knew I had to. I couldn't be responsible for his actions. I couldn't support his habit and I couldn't give him the stability of marriage or a roof over his head because these were the very things giving him the oxygen to feed his addiction. I had become like his mother, not his wife. I cleaned and washed for him, spoon-fed him when he shook so much he couldn't hold any cutlery, and ran upstairs countless times with gallons and gallons of water. I worried myself half to death that one day I'd come home and he'd be dead. Alcoholism is a disease; it's an illness that creeps in like a cancer affecting everything around you. I held on to the broken promises for so long and fought to find the husband I once knew, the perfect father… lost inside the glass.

I cried for weeks after he left and cursed alcohol as I passed the street bars and cafés of Benidorm as I watched the cheerful holidaymakers downing the pints for a euro as quick as the *camerero* could bring them to the table. I cursed the drink that came like a thief in the night and stole my wonderful husband.

In time, though, the tears eventually subsided and I forced myself to hold my head up high, convincing myself that no wife or partner could have done any more. It had taken me 15 years to realise all that, 15 years of second chances and frustration, heartache and broken promises.

Part of me believed that forcing Tom to stand on his own two feet would bring him to his senses and make him get help. However, part of me knew that would never happen. To this day he is still in denial.

My daughters and grandchildren were in Liverpool and I could count my friends in Benidorm on one hand, but I had a job to go to and a roof over my head. I picked up the pieces of my life and thought that things weren't all that bad and yes... the sun was shining too.

I faced up to reality and realised I might get a little lonely, just one person in one house. It was something I'd never ever experienced but I'd need to get used to it.

Crissy Rock was on her own, on her own in the land of the barking dogs...

CHAPTER TWENTY THREE

BENIDORM

I call Benidorm the land of the barking dogs and it is from here that I pen this penultimate chapter of my book. It seems morning, noon and night the dogs bark out their eardrum-shattering din and when one starts they all start. Dogs are kept outside in Spain because on the whole the weather is kind to them. The lucky ones have a kennel but not one of them on the entire Costa Blanca is soundproofed. Would you believe it?

The hours I keep, the neighbours must love me. By the time I stroll home into the quiet residential area of Benidorm a few hundred yards from where it all happens, Fido and Patcho and Pedro and Kiko are all fast asleep. I walk down the street I call home generally at around two in the morning, having finished my final spot around one and caught up on a cocoa or two to unwind. As I turn the corner to home, I am deafened by a silence that hits me like a hurricane and it reminds me to be quiet. I think of the countless nights and early mornings I have been woken by the perros de España and I sympathise with my Spanish neighbours.

And I try... I really do, honest to God. Some nights I have even been known to take my heels off, tiptoeing down the street like a criminal after curfew. But then something always sets them off: the gate, a door, a handle turning, my mobile phone ringing, a text even, an empty can of coke I've kicked, a taxi passing by. Then, all hell breaks out and it's like the gunfight at the canine corral.

When I first came to the Costa Blanca, I rented a villa some 10 miles outside Benidorm. It didn't seem too bad up there, but in Benidorm *everyone* has a dog that barks.

My first place on the Costa Blanca was in La Nucia. I had a four-bed villa with a pool. Tom had helped me pick the place where we would be living but obviously things didn't work out. When he moved back to the UK, I started to enjoy my freedom, and the peace and quiet. (Apart from the barking dogs.)

For the first time since I'd met B 28 years earlier, I only had me to worry about. Financially, I was doing well. I was performing at Valentines club seven nights a week and, although it wasn't lucrative, it allowed me to pay my rent, live how I wanted and I even managed to save a little. The second year I was in Benidorm, Margie Jones, Danielle and Melissa came for the summer holidays. I confess it was simply magical and I loved every minute. Although I still worked every night, because of my stage job, I could spend the other 22 hours a day with my wonderful grandchildren.

We played the Benidorm tourists' role to the full, swimming in the pool and the sea, building sandcastles and visiting the theme parks at Mundomar, Aqualandia and Terra Mitica. We even took the tourist train around Benidorm, which is called the Wally Trolley by the ex-pats for obvious reasons. Have you ever taken a look at the gormless faces of the average adult on that train and the men wearing Jesus sandals with socks? I'd want to run up to them and tell them, 'Jesus didn't wear socks with his sandals.' Well... I'm not ashamed to say it, but I was on that Wally Trolley with Danielle, Melissa and Margie more times than I'd care to remember and I didn't care... they loved it to bits.

At nights we'd dine early in the many restaurants round La Nucia and Benidorm or have a barbecue on the terrace and I'd tuck Danielle and Melissa up in bed before heading off out. As a treat, sometimes Margie would bring them down to see a little bit of my act at one of the early shows and I'd try my hardest not to swear on stage if I spotted them in the audience. I could see their faces beaming at me, tickled pink that it was their nan up there in the spotlight.

When they woke up the next morning, Nan would be there for them to give them their breakfast by the pool. Heaven on earth? Yes... I wish I could have sealed those precious weeks in a jar and screwed the top on so tight they would stay with me forever. All too soon, the holiday was over and I put on a brave face as I drove them to Alicante Airport. I'll never forget their little faces as they disappeared through the departure gate. They kept turning round and waving, smiling at me as if it was some sort of game. Then, as they got further and further away from me and nearer to airport security, there was the realisation that it wasn't a game and Nan wasn't playing nor would she be going back to Liverpool with them.

I burst into tears as they disappeared from sight and drove the car home in a torrential downpour... only it wasn't raining; the only windscreen wipers working were the Kleenex ones as I used half a box on the 45-minute journey home.

I realised after that holiday just how much I missed my family and my friends back home in Liverpool. I'd step out into a glorious Costa Blanca winter morning and worry about stupid things like whether they were warm enough back home. I especially missed Christmas with them and Santa and the markets, and cursed the fact that because of my occupation it was simply impossible to let my employers down and jump on a plane back to Liverpool for the festive period, the busiest time of the year.

I suppose I was lonely and yet I tried to convince myself that I'd been on my own most of my life. It's hard to describe... some days I moped around the house feeling sorry for myself and other days I appreciated the solitude. After all, you can be in a roomful of people and yet still be on your own.

I was feeling a little stale doing seven nights at Valentines and, although I tried to diversify my act with new material, some nights looking at the same four walls I began to get confused, wondering if I was beginning to repeat the same jokes and stories. I wasn't. I just thought I was. I cut down on my nights at Valentines and took more gigs at other clubs like Rockafellas, Gigolo's and Carriages and took on the bold move of doing more than one show per evening. At times, I began to get confused and on more than one occasion I would wander round Benidorm checking the chalkboards outside each venue to check the times. It worked up to a point but thank Christ it didn't rain much in Benidorm or I'd have been fucked!

The acting roles had all but dried up and I calculated that it had been nearly three years since I'd had paid work as an actress. Reality-TV shows like *Big Brother* had killed off the new drama productions and made-for-TV films. Times had changed, everyone was fixated on *Pop Idol* and *Celebrity Love*

Island and fly-on-the-wall documentaries. I didn't like that trend, but there was absolutely nothing I could do about it. I wasn't too concerned though, as I had regular employment and limited overheads.

I needed a little break from the Costa Blanca though. Shortly after Christmas and New Year, I checked my bank balance and booked a ticket to the place I'd always wanted to go to as a child: New York.

I arrived in JFK Airport at 10 in the evening in early March 2006, and as I stepped out into the New York air I couldn't help but cry. Stupid... yes, I know. But I had been fascinated for years by the story of the *Titanic* and its intended destination. Granddad, our own Ancient Mariner, had told me that story, and about the iceberg, during our times on the Pier Head. He had described the poor souls who froze in the water, mourning how they'd never see the Statue of Liberty or New York's grand City Hall. As a teenager, I had devoured the pictures of New York in magazines and books and, when I learned to read, I took book after book from the shelves of my local library and absorbed every word.

And finally I was here. Tomorrow I would see those sights and more. I'd take in some shows on Broadway too. As I got to my hotel by Macy's, I was like a dog with two bones. Apart from getting electrocuted: every bloody door was steel and every carpet made of nylon. Each time I touched a door or a table I got a static electric shock.

I slept well, at peace with myself and more than a little self-congratulatory that here I was in the Big Apple under my own steam. At 10 the following morning, just before I left my hotel room for the day, I took a phone call from reception asking me to call my agent Triona Adams, who had telephoned in the early hours of the morning.

'I'm in New York, Triona,' I told her like a schoolgirl. 'Don't tell me – I have to come home, don't I?'

Triona explained I'd been offered a part in Lynda La Plante's TV series *Trial & Retribution*, and I had to call Lynda's office immediately. My heart sank and, after jotting down the number, I replaced the receiver. This could only happen to Crissy Rock: on my first holiday for as long as I could remember, in the city of my dreams that I'd wanted to visit ever since I'd been a snotty-nosed kid in Liverpool 8, the great hand of fate had intervened yet again and fucked it up!

I did what any self-respecting individual would have done in similar circumstances: cried my eyes out as I looked out of my bedroom window on to 7th Avenue and the never-ending lines of traffic. When I recovered, I picked up the phone, punched in the UK code and called Lynda La Plante's office in London. I'm glad I did. 'The job's safe,' the office girl told me. 'No audition. Lynda wants you to play the part. There's no one else in for it, Lynda said the part is made for you.'

'But I'll need to audition,' I stuttered.

'No audition, Miss Rock, the part's yours.'

I literally ran from the hotel foyer into the bright but freezing cold New York sunshine, even more eager to have the time of my life. A part in a Lynda La Plante production on my return seemed to be more than I could ever have wished for. At last, the big man in the clouds had answered at least one or two of my prayers.

The thought of working for Lynda was wonderful and the whole experience lived up to my expectations. On the face of it, the financial rewards seemed more than generous but, of course, unlike most of the other actors and actresses, I didn't have a place in London to stay. I had to pay for my own accommodation for two months and my flights and travel expenses. Then of course there were the agents' fees and tax and national insurance. Do not be under any misconception that all actresses and actors are millionaires. I walked away with less than £3,000 for the time I spent on set. I'd lost more money from gigs in Benidorm. Having said all that, it was a fantastic two months and will live in my heart forever. As I've said before, they are memories and memories are priceless.

* * *

Back in Benidorm, I resumed my cabaret duties. The phone started ringing again, and I fell back into my normal routine with performances at Rockafellas and Carriages. I also took on a new spot at the UK Cabaret Bar, a huge venue that was almost full every evening throughout the year.

The only cloud on the horizon came from my daughters. They would call to tell me about Tom and the mess he was in. Hayley told me that he said he'd made the biggest mistake of his life, but I shrugged it off… I'd heard it all before. Then one morning at about 3.40, the phone rang. It was Tom. It had been exactly two years since I had moved to Benidorm, and nearly a year after I'd packed Tom back off to Liverpool. Claiming to be sober, he told me that he wanted to try again with our relationship, and that if I gave it a go he would never take another drink in his life.

At first I wondered why he'd called at stupid o'clock but he seemed to sense my thought pattern and told me he hadn't been able to sleep. I was incoherent and sleepy, and he begged me to give him one last chance. I said I'd think about it when I'd had a good sleep. Sleep? That was a joke. I never slept a wink and was up at first light drinking coffee.

A few hours later, Tom called again. 'Please take me back,' he said. He wanted to come to Benidorm just for a holiday, told me he'd seen the light, and if he could just fly over he would prove that he didn't need a single drink. If he could stay sober in Benidorm, he could stay sober anywhere in the world. He claimed he'd changed, realising what he'd lost, and realising how much he loved me and wanted me back. I told him to give me a few weeks to think about it and if he still felt the same he could come over. I emphasised to him that it was only a holiday – no promises – and, if I were to take him back, he'd have to be sober… One slip and he was history.

I was feeling confused, though. I'd been on my own quite a while and had to admit I was enjoying the peace of mind, and the peace and quiet that comes with it. Part of me didn't want to go back to having to think about others, where they were, what they wanted to eat, what time they'd be home. I thought back to my trip to New York and what a great time I'd had. I'd woken up one morning and booked the flights and hotel on a whim. I wouldn't have been able to do that if I hadn't been single. So why was there another part of me telling me that the love with Tom wouldn't take an awful lot of rekindling? Why was something deep down inside telling me that I was still in love with this man who was making so many promises?

I shrugged it off. He'd probably fall off the wagon before long and be back to his old ways. The phone call would never happen. My friend from Glasgow, Maureen Mathis, had planned a trip to Benidorm in October 2006. A friend of hers had let her down and she was about to cancel the trip because she had no one to come with. 'Don't be stupid,' I said. 'Stay with me, we'll have a great time. As long as you realise I need to go to work for a few hours each evening, things will work out great. I've a two-bed apartment. You'll have a room to yourself.'

BENIDORM

Maureen was still a little reluctant but I persisted. She booked the flights the same day.

Two weeks before Maureen was due to arrive, I did receive that call from Tom and he wanted to fly out to see me the following week. I explained all about Maureen but he didn't mind, and even suggested it might be better to have a little company around. What could I say? Before he hung up, he reaffirmed his promises all over again.

Tom had been staying with me for a week when Maureen arrived, and I made up my bed on the settee giving Tom and Maureen their own bedrooms. (That's me all over.) I explained the situation with Tom to Maureen and apologised, but she told me not to be stupid. For a week, all was well, and the three of us spent a lot of time together. We went into Benidorm, and to the markets, and on day trips to Calpe and Altea. Tom had been as good as his word and even when we had gone into Benidorm in the evenings he drank nothing but coke. Part of me almost wished he would take to the drink again as my emotions were shot to bits.

I was seeing the old Tom once again, the gentleman, the man with a little compassion, a smile instead of a sneer, a kind word here and there. Towards the end of the second week, I even started to wonder if it might work again. But it was a Sunday morning at the El Cisne market when I began to notice the familiar signs. El Cisne market is a *rastro*, a Benidorm car-boot fair but on a huge scale with bands and paella and, of course, bars. It was quite a hot morning for the time of year and Tom, ever the gentleman, kept disappearing into the bars to bring Maureen and me cool drinks.

I should have noticed something was up, but at first I didn't. Our drinks were always in cans or bottles and his was always in a red Coca Cola plastic cup. I should have remembered my schooling at Al-Anon: alcoholics are clever people, and they excel in the art of concealment. We were there for a few hours and eventually decided to walk up the street to the car. Just before the end of the market, there was a bar and Tom dived in, before appearing a few moments later with his plastic cup and a bottle of water. I asked him if he had had a drink.

He went off the deep end calling me all the bastards under the sun, saying I was doubting him and generally using the F-word several times in each sentence. Maureen's jaw nearly hit the deck at the language pouring from his mouth. But I had my answer: Tom only spoke like this when he was drunk. Good old vodka... his colourless, tasteless, odourless friend. And at that point I realised Tom must have been drinking vodka and cokes the whole day long. He had simply been topping himself up.

It all fell into place. I remembered the occasions when he'd been only too keen to run out to the shops for a paper or some bread, and remembered when the five-minute trip out for the *Daily Mirror* had taken the best part of an hour. And of course, when he returned, I'd passed a comment along the lines that he must have been printing the bloody thing and we'd all had a little giggle.

But now I knew for sure... he'd lied... I'd spent all those years with a man who couldn't give a shit about me. And I wanted to cry right there and then as I pushed the car key into the lock and opened the door. Maureen climbed into the back as Tom struggled with the passenger door before eventually settling in the seat. He was still cursing. 'I'm fucking fed up with you questioning everything I do.' I ignored him. As I started the car engine one of my CDs automatically kicked in. He glanced over at me. 'This one of your fancy man's fucking tapes, is it?'

'What?'

'I bet you've had a fucking ball since you've been on your own.'

His face was twisted, the sneer was back. I pressed eject, released the CD and threw it out of the open window on the street and drove off. He didn't answer and all I could think of was Maureen in the back. At the next set of traffic lights, we stopped at a red and he started ranting and raving again. Before they changed, he opened the door and jumped out.

'I'm off,' he shouted. 'You couldn't give a fuck about me.'

I shouted at him to get in the car; the lights had changed to green.

'I'm not getting in that fucking car, fuck off home to your perfect little bachelor pad with your fancy men's music.'

The cars behind me were getting impatient and their horns were blaring, but Tom was oblivious.

'Get in the bloody car,' I shouted. 'We'll be arrested.'

Tom looked around and obviously felt a little uncomfortable.

A man in the car behind was calling him a *jilipoya*, a Spanish swear word which, literally translated, means a fat prick. I went on at him to get in the car and, if I remember rightly, Maureen offered a few words of encouragement too. Tom reluctantly climbed back in and we breathed a sigh of relief. But our relief was short-lived. As soon as I pulled up outside the apartment, Tom stormed off in the opposite direction effing and blinding and I knew he was off out on a bender.

Maureen never said a word until we had walked into the apartment. She looked at me, hand on hips. 'How on earth do you put up with that?'

I asked myself the same question.

Tom came back seven hours later and he was off the map, bouncing off the walls of the narrow corridor. He could hardly walk or talk and the whole room reeked of alcohol as he spoke. He came in abusive, on the defensive and of course blamed everything on me. I refused to get drawn into the argument and left for work with Maureen soon after.

I was performing at the UK Cabaret Bar. It was jam-packed and as Maureen settled herself on a stool by the bar I made my way to the dressing room to get ready.

When I came off stage, I walked towards Maureen. She was in tears. 'What's wrong?' I asked. 'What's the matter?'

Maureen wiped at the tears, and it took a few minutes before she could speak. 'Look at these people, Crissy.'

I looked to where she was pointing. I shrugged my shoulders. 'What about them?'

'You made them laugh.'

It sounded such a silly statement. 'Yes, Maureen, that's my job. I'm a comedienne.'

Maureen's tears flowed once again. 'You made them laugh, Crissy. After the day you've put in, you've made them laugh. How, Crissy...? How did you do that?'

* * *

Tom was full of apologies the next day. He said he'd had a little slip and it wouldn't happen again. I said nothing. A few days later, Maureen headed home, but, over the next two weeks, Tom would slip quite a few times. He wasn't permanently drunk but a five- or six-hour drinking session followed by 16 hours in bed became the norm, as if we were back home in Croxdale Park. He had his feet well and truly under the table again. Or so he thought. He acted as if everything was just hunky-dory.

We flew back to England together in early November, as I was about to perform in panto in Liverpool. Tom had kindly suggested I could stay in his flat in St Helens. I decided it made sense, as paying for a hotel for eight weeks in Liverpool would more than eat up my wages for playing one of the ugly sisters in *Cinderella*. The first week we were rehearsing and after the second full day I returned to the flat at St Helens. I didn't have a key. I knocked and knocked on the door for some time before I realised that either Tom wasn't in or that he was sleeping somewhere behind the closed door in an alcoholic coma. To make matters worse, it was pouring with rain.

I was beginning to panic a little as all my clothes, credit cards and money were in Tom's flat. I rang the house from my mobile. No answer. I slept in the car. I had no option as it was too late to knock anybody up at that time of night. I rang Tom's flat all day and still there was no reply. I made a call to British Telecom suggesting the line might be faulty. The operator did a few checks and called me back, confirming that the line was perfect.

I went back to the flat again that night, and the following night too, but there was no sign of life anywhere. I wasn't worried – I knew exactly where he was, and what he was up to. I was furious, though – I was begging a bed each night at the homes of friends and family, going to rehearsals in the same clothes day after day, washing my underwear each night and, of course, I was running out of cash. I went to the bank to try to get new cards but there was little I could do as my passport and driving licence were locked up behind the door of a flat in St Helens. I had more subs than a naval fleet.

Tom finally answered the door on the fifth day. He was stinking of alcohol and slurring his speech. He acted as if nothing was wrong and even offered me a coffee. We had a row and I asked him why the hell he hadn't called me in five days. I looked at his face. He was puzzled. I could see exactly what he was thinking: he was thinking, 'Five days?' His bender had lasted five days but clearly he'd lost two or three of them along the way. He furrowed his brow. 'Five days?'

'Five fucking days,' I screamed. 'Look at my clothes, I've been wearing the same bloody knickers for nearly a week and you couldn't give a fuck, you selfish prick.'

Yes, I was angry, but, more than that, I was hurt. He'd conned me, set me up begging for yet another last chance and I'd buckled and given him it. He stood there shrugging his shoulders and even at that point as I ranted at him he still thought that life was sweet, that he hadn't done anything wrong. I began gathering my things together and he had the nerve to ask where I was going. I remained quiet. If I'd spoken, I might have hit him. And, even as I threw everything in my suitcase and zipped it up, he spoke as if I was just taking a couple of days out to cool off. He asked me when I'd be back, he even asked me how the rehearsals were going. The last thing he said to me as I walked out of the door was: 'You're supposed to love me.'

I turned to face him and said, 'I always did.'

After the eight weeks of pantomime, I returned to the Costa Blanca. I shed a few tears in the taxi to the airport, but those tears were strictly for my grandchildren and daughters, not Tom. I vowed I would never ever shed another tear for him, no matter what.

Luckily, an exciting new opportunity for me had arisen back in Benidorm. One evening as I came off stage after doing my act, I was approached by two men. One of them introduced himself as Derren Litten, a huge man who was aged about 30. Speaking quietly but confidently, he told me all about a comedy series he had written, and said he wanted me to star in it. What the hell, I thought, it felt right and I immediately took to Derren. We had a drink, he told me a little about the plot, and said the whole show was situated in Benidorm, so I would have no problem with accommodation or anything like that.

'Brilliant,' I said. 'Count me in.'

If I remember rightly, we shook hands and I asked him what it was called.

'*Benidorm*,' Derren replied with a grin.

And the rest, as they say, is history.

***

The first series of *Benidorm* aired on ITV from 1 February to 8 March 2007, and was even nominated in the Best Sitcom category of the 2008 BAFTA Awards. This was a measure of the success of the first series so it was no surprise when a second series was commissioned. I play the character Janey York, hotel manageress-cum-receptionist-cum-resident quizmistress.

Not many people are aware that, for each day's filming, we must be in make-up by six o'clock in the morning, a schedule which plays havoc with my work schedule. Some of my comedy gigs run on until the early hours of the morning, so it's quite tough rolling into bed at two in the morning, then being woken by the alarm at five. However, once we are on set, the tiredness fades and the fun begins. It sounds slushy but we really are a great team, one big happy family from the top stars of the show to the wardrobe, catering, lighting and extras. When the first episode aired, I trooped down to the Geordie bar with a big gang of the extras and we watched it on the big screen. It was better than any premiere in Leicester Square, I can tell you.

Benidorm has really taken off and built up a real following, particularly in the UK. I'm hoping the fourth series will begin filming soon and, even though I know I will be mentally drained by the end of the production, I can't wait for it to start and to meet up with everyone again.

It was when the first series was being shot that I received a rather strange email, which had been forwarded to me by my agent. Apparently, a secret admirer had watched one of my Benidorm club gigs and said that he hadn't laughed as much in years, but, as I walked offstage, he believed he had looked into the saddest eyes he had ever seen. He said in his email that he would give £1,000 to charity if my agent could arrange for him to sit down with me and have a cup of tea.

Jesus Christ, I thought, I have a stalker. Piss off, you sad bastard, and get a life.

I deleted the email and hoped I would hear no more from my secret admirer.

It was several months later. I had lent one of my cameras to a so-called friend who did a runner with it back to England. It was an expensive camera but, more importantly, it carried a memory card with photographs of my father's funeral. I wanted the camera, and more so the memory card, back. I left several messages on my elusive friend's phone but he would not return my call. I began asking individuals and acquaintances in Benidorm whether they knew of anyone in his area who had the balls to knock on the person's door and ask for my camera back.

Eventually, a month or two later, someone approached me after my club show and promised me the matter was in hand. After a few days, I received a phone call from a chap with a gorgeous accent saying that he had my camera.

'Fantastic,' I said. 'It's very precious to me. Can you make sure you send it over special delivery and let me know how much I owe you?' I couldn't thank him enough.

Fourteen hours later, I was sitting in my lounge doing a little painting when I received a phone call. It was the camera man. He was sitting in a café in Benidorm with my precious cargo – complete with that memory card. I didn't believe him and asked him why... how? He said he realised how important it was to me so he thought he'd make sure it got here safely. I burst out crying and told my knight in shining armour that I couldn't thank him enough. When I asked him if there was anything I could do to repay him, he smiled and said, 'Yes, you can let me take you for dinner.'

'OK,' I said, 'that's fair enough, but let me take you out.'

He wouldn't have it, insisted it was his treat and he told me we could go anywhere in Benidorm that I wanted. We sat in a Chinese restaurant near to the Rincon area of Benidorm and enjoyed a €4 menu of the day'. As we finished the final course, he told me about the email he had sent to my agent many months ago and mentioned the £1,000 that he had been willing to give to charity.

Fucking hell! I nearly choked on my chicken fried rice. I was sitting opposite my 'stalker', only this 'stalker' was nothing of the sort. He was kind, pleasant and loving and – dare I say it – even quite handsome. He flew back to England that night, and I sent him a text to wish him a safe journey around the time I estimated that he'd be going into the airport departure lounge. When he landed at the airport, he called me to say he was home. He never stalked or pestered me, but, over the weeks that followed, we texted each other from time to time.

I didn't see him for several weeks. It was on the opening night of my next pantomime that I walked into my dressing room at Liverpool's Royal Court, and my eyes locked on to the biggest bouquet I had ever seen. My automatic reaction was that I had walked into the wrong dressing room. I never got chocolates or flowers on an opening night, but, as I read the card attached to the bouquet, I realised that I was in the right dressing room, and that the flowers really were for me. The card read: 'Crissy, I am behind you all the way and you know who these are from.'

My secret admirer was in the audience. He came to meet me after the performance and wanted to take me out, but I explained that I was on my way to meet my brother Jason who was playing in a tribute band called the Mersey Beatles at the Cavern Club.

His face fell, and now he was the one with the saddest eyes in the world.

'Don't be silly,' I said. 'You can come along too.'

And within 10 minutes we were in town outside the Cavern Club. We walked into the club and I made a beeline for Jason. For a full five minutes, I forgot all about the man standing behind me as I was engrossed in conversation with Jason and his band members. I was so used to being on my own, but suddenly I remembered the man I was with. I offered my apologies, took him by the hand and guided him into our group as I introduced him. Our hands would remain that way for the rest of the evening. Who said romance is dead?

So there you have it – a little romance has entered Crissy Rock's life. It works well; he lives in England and I still live here in Benidorm, but every few weeks we get together, have a few drinks and enjoy the occasional night on the town. I don't know if it will go any further than that – we'll just have to wait and see – but I'm happy that he is in my life.

And when he steps off the bus to see me, I always have my *Shirley Valentine* moment. I picture the scene as Joe is walking towards her. She's sitting at a table on the beach. She's changed, he doesn't recognise her. He walks right past her at first but eventually comes over to her. It's a fantastic scene. And then there are the closing lines of the film, as uttered by its star, Pauline Collins:

'Oh, I hope he stays for a while. He needs a holiday. He needs to feel the sun on his back and to be in water that's as deep as forever.'

I love that scene. I love those lines.

AND FINALLY...

This project was never intended to be a book. It started off with me, Crissy Rock, just pounding at the keys on a PC in a desperate attempt to clear the torment and demons from my inner self. I had a crazy theory that, if I could get these dark thoughts transferred on to paper, somehow I would be miraculously exorcised. Those areas of my brain that housed all those dark thoughts would be freed up again, and I could replace them with more pleasant things. In a way it worked; the psychologists call it closure, I believe.

When I'd written about a particularly disturbing chapter about my life, and I'd print out my half-dozen pages of memories, I would concentrate hard, to will those thoughts from my head on to the sheets of paper. I'd convince myself this wasn't a duplication process; it was a transfer.

Next I'd sit in the garden, reading what I'd written over and over again, often on the brink of tears. Then, finally, I'd set the

257

pages on fire, imagining that the words on those sheets were floating away into the night sky and would soon be gone forever. My neighbours at the time must have thought I was a raving lunatic.

A friend once asked me, if I could be reincarnated, who I would like to come back as. Without a moment's hesitation, I replied, 'As myself, of course.' My friend gave me the most peculiar look; she was well aware of my past history and all the suffering I'd gone through, all the abuse, violence and alcoholism that had torn my family apart. But I meant it because, in spite of everything, my life has been filled with many blessings and I still have the most precious gift of all. That gift is called life. I think anyone who has battled cancer and won will know exactly what I am talking about. Some people are not that lucky. I have taken this gift of life and held on to it with both hands.

As you have read, at times my life has been like a fairground ride. At times I've felt so sick I wanted the ride to stop. I was scared and unsure what the next spin of the ride would bring. But at other times, just around the next corner, the ride would give me the most amazing feeling and I would want it to go on forever.

Many times I have thanked whoever it is up there who arranged and planned the map of my life, but above all else I have thanked him for giving me the strength and faith to face up to the things that have happened in my life and the courage to continue. Whatever shit life throws at me, I stand tall, puff out my chest and shout, 'Bring it on because I'm going to be just fine. You won't ever defeat me.'

I am also a believer that some people come in and out of your life as earth angels and that they touch you and stay with you for a while then disappear. At the time, you may be forgiven for wondering why they are here, but eventually you will discover, perhaps many years later, that they all served a purpose, no matter how insignificant it seemed.

I have never been one for self-pity. It's all so easy to just sit there and cry and say, 'Oh, poor me,' but what does that ever achieve?

Sadly, we cannot change our past; believe me, I've wanted to turn back that clock many times and take a different turn or direction. The only thing we can change or influence is in our future, and the future in us starts right now.

I've cried so many tears over the years, and I was the biggest people-pleaser in the world. Because of the way my early life had worked out, I felt I needed people to like me because I didn't like me. I spent all my time and energy trying to make people happy and make them laugh when all the time I was dying and crying inside. Those tears, however, have been the water that has fed and nurtured the roots of my soul, strengthened me and transformed me into the sort of person I am today.

If we spend so much of our lives trying to love and please other people that we forget about valuing and loving ourselves, that's when we become lost and empty. Then, as a way of defence, we start to blame others for those feelings because we feel hurt and let down. It's very difficult in any relationship when you feel that the other person hasn't given back the same level of love or understanding. Some people are givers in life and some are takers and, no matter how hard we try, we will never change that.

I look at things very differently now. I was abused but I survived; I was raped but I survived; and my first husband beat me to within an inch of my life. But I survived. I have a beautiful daughter Tracy, not the ideal circumstances under which to conceive, but even so I had a beautiful baby girl and wouldn't have changed her for the world. I love her dearly and hold on to the good memories of our times together... there are so many.

Although my first marriage was one of continued violence until the day we were divorced, if I had never met B, I wouldn't have had my second daughter Hayley, and perhaps I wouldn't have found the strength within me to fight for my dignity and self-respect.

My second marriage ended in divorce too, but then again I try to take the positives from it. Without Tom's help, I would never have found it in myself to learn to read and I thank him for that. Although I tried everything to stop his drinking, I now realise that only an alcoholic can do that. Drink came in like a thief in the night and stole my husband from me. That period of my life was undoubtedly the worst. I watched the man I loved drive me and my daughters to the very edge of insanity. Alcoholism is a disease, a cancer of the soul, and letting Tom go was the hardest thing I ever did. My only regret is that I didn't do it earlier, before it affected our family so badly. As the children grew into teenagers, they didn't understand why I was never there, why I had to work every day God gave me, and why they had to walk around on eggshells all the time. They weren't even allowed to bring their friends to the house because their father was lying around drunk most of the time.

Yet, from all those tough experiences, I grew stronger still, gaining knowledge, wisdom and, of course, yet more experience. Without that, I would never have met my dearest friends at Al-Anon, nor found the true meaning of the serenity prayer.

AND FINALLY...

God grant me the serenity
to accept the things I cannot change;
the courage to change the things I can;
and wisdom to know the difference.

I now have the serenity to accept the things that have happened. I found the courage to change it and I now have the wisdom not to let it get to me.

So I got through it all in my own way. Over the years, I have learned to forgive and forget, and by forgiving I am not weighed down with the anguish and the hatred of it all.

I still believe in the magic of Christmas. I see that magic now in the faces of my grandchildren and I still make time to release the child within myself, the child I was once not allowed to be.

I collect dolls and musical boxes, and I love toys and am not embarrassed or ashamed to sit and play with them whenever I feel the child in me wants to come back out and play.

I still have some little bouts of depression but reassure myself that we all get down sometimes. Then I see someone who is severely disabled, perhaps wheelchair-bound. I watch the anguish in their face, sometimes they twist and turn, their arms flailing, the head lolling from side to side as if to say, 'Where am I? What am I doing here?' And after I dismiss the urge to rush over and comfort them, I realise how lucky I am, that, by the grace of God, I am not that person.

I am not a psychiatrist nor do I have a magic formula that I can pass on to anyone. However, if I could give one piece of advice to anyone who has suffered from the sort of abuse or torment I've been through, I would say: Let go of the past... let go of the ghosts, the gremlins and the demons and look to the future. It has taken me nearly 50 years to get to know myself, to understand what life is all about and those years have gone by so very quickly. Giving advice is easy; it's taking the advice that's the hard bit and we can all dwell on the past and stand still. We can all live in the world of could have, should have, would have, but it will get us nowhere, I promise you.

My brother Brian is a schizophrenic now; in his mind he still hears the voice of the Ancient Mariner. I wish I could climb inside my brother's head and fight those voices for him, convince him that they cannot hurt him any more. Poor Brian – our granddad had inflicted years of physical abuse on him, and even strangled him at times until he passed out.

We all have different ways of coping and some cope better than others. I learned to move the pain by cutting myself. The physical pain of self-harming was not as painful as the mental torture and anguish I was suffering inside. Cutting into my flesh was like cutting my grandfather's grip away from me. Releasing the blood was like releasing a valve on a pressure cooker, and watching the blood flow was, to my mind, like watching the pain leave me.

There's an old saying: you can't beat experience. I can relate to that, maybe the secret of life comes with age. There's a lot more to life than material possessions and PlayStations, iPhones and DVD players. With life's experience comes an inner peace and an optimistic approach to the future. After many years on this small planet, I have learned to love myself. If someone doesn't like me, then fuck them; I'm not worried and I won't lose any sleep. They can deal with it because I don't have to.

Even the Ancient Mariner cannot hurt me any more because I will not let him. Memories of my past come and go. I have learned to keep the bad memories at bay or at least have managed to get them out of my head quickly because they are not welcome in my life any more. The good memories I hold on to and nurture, and I talk about them to my friends and family at every possible chance I get.

Eventually, it seems that you have a lot more good memories than bad ones and you start thinking that life's deck of cards has been a good one. I look at my hand and, while it hasn't exactly been a royal flush, there are plenty of kings and aces in there.

Maybe the big key to life's secret was written in the Monty Python song 'Always Look On The Bright Side Of Life'. Who knows? But there again it's a bloody nice place to start!

I once looked into the mirror and all I could see was a frightened young girl, tears running down her cheeks, a picture of confusion and fear. Then, as I got older, I saw the face of a battered young woman with black eyes and broken teeth. I stopped looking in the mirror because I was frightened of the worthless individual that stared back at me. That's what I thought, that's what I felt like... worthless and pathetic. I felt that way because the love I'd been given was abusive love. So I stopped looking in the mirror and started looking inside Crissy Rock instead.

Learning to read properly was one of the greatest gifts my life could ever have given me. Once again, I must thank my ex-husband Tom for helping me believe in myself, and helping me to come to terms with the fact that I could do it if I really wanted to. If someone had told me 25 years ago that not only would I write a book but that I would also manage to actually get it published, I would have laughed in their face.

Life is a strange journey, one that we sometimes stumble on blindly. In a way the completion of this book has also been one of life's journeys. I'm not a great writer, I know that, and yet with a little help from Scotty and a huge slice of self-belief I've managed to pull it together. At times, it has been very difficult for me, a bitter-sweet experience opening up things that I never wanted to ever think about or live through again. And at times many months have passed when I have been unable to go near the keyboard.

As I close this chapter of my life, I am 51 years of age and turning over new pages of a new chapter every single day. I cannot wait for each page I turn to begin. Now this heart within in me burns not with pain, or anguish, or fear, but with life and love and self-worth.

My final few thoughts concern the hundreds of thousands of people who have come to see me perform my comedy since I arrived here in Benidorm. People come back year after year. They are my friends who've supported me simply by putting their bums on the seats and laughing at me and with me. They've brought me presents and even birthday cakes. They are like one big surrogate family.

My dear friends from Belfast, Dee and Margaret Anderson, are regular visitors, but there's also David and Mary from Wales. They never miss a year in Benidorm and, when they are here, they come to see me perform two or three times. How nice is that? It's that huge surrogate family that gives me the strength to carry on. They bring me inner peace.

I hope you, my dear reader, manage to find your own peace, your own love and your own self-worth. I hope you have enjoyed our brief journey together and managed to pull the tiniest little something, no matter how small, from the pages in this book.

If you have then it has been worth writing.

God bless you.

xxxxxxx